**Spelling and Writing**

In this fifth book in the Spelling and Writing Together series, children learn to identify and use nouns, subjects, and verbs in sentences. Then they replace nouns with pronouns, combine short sentences with conjunctions, and add adjectives and adverbs to make their writing more interesting and more informative. In other lessons, children learn how to start paragraphs with topic sentences and add details to support the main idea. They practice separating fact from opinion, explaining their own opinions, writing from different points of view, and organizing several paragraphs of information.

# Table of Contents

# Glossary

**Adjectives.** Words that describe nouns and pronouns.

**Adverb.** Words that tell something about a verb.

**Apostrophe.** A punctuation mark that shows possession (Kim's hat) or takes the place of missing letters in a word (isn't).

**Digraph.** Two consonant letters pronounced as one consonant sound.

**Fact.** A true statement. Something that can be proved.

**Homophones.** Words that sound alike but have different spellings and meanings.

**Joining Words** (Conjunctions). Words that join sentences orcombine ideas.

**Metaphor.** A comparison without the words like or as.

**Noun.** A word that names a person, place, or thing.

**Opinion.** What someone thinks or believes.

**Paragraph.** A group of sentences that tells about one main idea.

**Plural.** A word that refers to more than one thing.

**Prefix.** One or two syllables added to the beginning of a word to change its meaning.

**Pronoun.** A word that can be used in place of a noun.

**Question.** A sentence that asks something.

**Simile.** A comparison using the words like or as.

**Singular.** A word that refers to only one thing.

**Subject.** A word or several words that tell whom or what a sentence is about.

**Suffix.** One or two syllables added to the end of a word.

**Synonym.** A word that means the same thing as another word.

**Verb.** The action word in a sentence; the word that tells what something does or that something exists.

Name: _____

# Recognizing The Short Vowels

The short vowels are:  /**a**/ as in **a**nd          /**e**/ as in f**e**d and br**ea**d
                        /**i**/ as in p**i**n          /**o**/ as in d**o**g
                        /**u**/ as in s**u**n and c**o**me

**Directions:** Use words from the word box in these exercises.

| punch | rob | pet | stock | lack | dent |
|-------|-----|-----|-------|------|------|
| brag | scrub | rinse | flip | | |

1. Write each word under its vowel sound.

   /a/            /e/            /i/            /o/            /u/

_____    _____    _____    _____    _____

_____    _____    _____    _____    _____

2. Say the word on the left. Then circle the two other words in that row that have the same
   vowel sound.

**Like this:**

| **rob** | sock | room | robe | knot |
|---------|------|------|------|------|
| **brag** | bring | brand | tack | brake |
| **dent** | breath | breathe | deer | bend |
| **rinse** | rink | dim | tents | force |
| **stock** | stuck | soak | stop | jog |
| **punch** | lunch | month | moon | match |

(sock is circled)

3. Finish these sentences, using a word with the vowel sound given. Use each word from the
   word box only once.

Because of the strike, there was a /a/ _____ of /o/ _____ on the store shelves.

The /u/ _____ tasted so bad I had to /i/ _____ my mouth out.

After my bike did a /i/ _____ in the mud, I had to /u/ _____ my clothes.

Name: _____

# Deciding Which Noun Is The Subject

A noun is a word that names a person, place, or thing. Here are some nouns: Andy, Mrs. Henderson, doctor, child, house, school, yard, desk, pencil, apple, shirt, dog, freedom, country.

Often a noun is the subject of a sentence. The subject tells whom or what the sentence is about. In this sentence the subject is **Sara**: Sara drank some punch. A sentence can have several nouns, but they are not all subjects. The nouns are underlined in the sentences below. The noun that is the subject of this sentence is circled.

(Benny) caught a huge <u>fish</u> in a small <u>net</u>.

**Directions:** Underline each noun in the sentences below. Then circle the noun that is the subject of the sentence.

1. Anna bragged about her big brother.

2. The car has a dent in the fender.

3. This school lacks spirit now.

4. The cook scrubbed the pots and pans.

5. The quarter flipped onto the floor.

6. My sister rinsed her hair in the sink.

7. Our neighbor has twelve pets.

8. The boy punched his pillow in anger.

9. Two people robbed the store on the corner.

10. A farmer stocks this pond with fish.

**Directions:** Each sentence below has two subjects. Underline all the nouns, as you did above. Then circle both subjects.

**Like this:** (Joe) and (Peter) walked to <u>school</u>.

1. Apples and peaches grow in different seasons.

2. The chair and table matched the other furniture.

Name: _____

# Using Math On Words

**Directions:** Add and subtract sounds to make new words. The spelling of the whole word may change.

**Like this:**

stock - /o/ + /i/ = <u>stick</u>

1. punch - /u/ + /i/ = _____

2. lack + /b/ = _____

3. flip - /i/ + /o/ = _____

4. rob - /o/ + /i/ = _____

5. lack - /a/ + /i/ = _____

6. scrub - /k/ + /h/ = _____

7. pet - /e/ + /a/ = _____

8. scrub - /sk/ = _____

9. flip - /fl/ + /gr/ = _____

10. lack - /a/ + /u/ = _____

11. rinse + /p/ = _____

12. net - /e/ + /u/ = _____

13. rob - /o/ + /u/ = _____

14. brag - /b/ + /d/ = _____

15. flip - /i/ + /a/ = _____

16. scrub - /ru/ + /a/ = _____

17. lack - /a/ + /o/ = _____

18. stock - /o/ + /u/ = _____

# Finding Subjects And Verbs

A verb is the action word in a sentence. It tells what the subject does (for example: **build, live, express, fasten**) or that it exists **(is, are, was, were,** and others). Remember that a verb can be two or more words: <u>is walking</u>, <u>are listening</u>, <u>was writing</u>, <u>were learning</u>.

**Directions:** Underline the subject and verb in each sentence below. Write **S** over the subject and **V** over the verb. If the verb is two words, mark them both.

**Like this:**    <u>Dennis</u> <u>was drinking</u> some punch.          The <u>punch</u> <u>was</u> too sweet.

1. Hayley brags about her dog all the time.

2. Mrs. Thomas scrubbed the dirt off her car.

3. Then her son rinsed the soap off.

4. The teacher was flipping through the cards.

5. Jenny's rabbit was hungry and thirsty.

6. Your science report lacks a title.

7. Mike and Chris are stocking the shelves with cans of soup.

8. The accident caused a huge dent in our car.

Just as sentences can have two subjects, they can have two verbs.

**Like this:**    Jennifer <u>fed</u> her dog and <u>gave</u> him clean water.

**Directions:** Underline all the subjects and verbs in these sentences. Write **S** over the subjects and **V** over the verbs.

1. The worker scrubbed and rinsed the floor.

2. The men came and stocked the lake with fish.

3. Someone broke a window and robbed the store.

4. Carrie punched a hole in the paper and threaded yarn through the hole.

5. Julie and Pat turned their bikes around and went home.

# Knowing When To Double Consonants

Many people aren't sure whether to double the last consonant of verbs when they add endings such as **-ing** and **-ed**. Is it **riped** or **ripped**? Here is the rule: Double the last consonant of verbs that have short vowel sounds (like all the verbs in the word box on page 1) and end with only one consonant letter (like **some** of them).

Thus, **rip** becomes **ripped** and **beg** becomes **begging**. However, we don't double the last consonant in **rock**. Even though it has a short vowel, it ends with two consonant letters: **ck**. So **rock** becomes **rocked**.

**Directions:** Add **-ed** to the verbs below. Be careful about which last consonants you double. Remember that when a verb ends with **e**, drop the **e** before adding an ending (taste, tasted, tasting).

**Like this:**

| | | | |
|---|---|---|---|
| top | _____topped_____ | rip | _____ripped_____ |
| pet | _____ | punch | _____ |
| rob | _____ | rinse | _____ |
| brag | _____ | stock | _____ |
| scrub | _____ | lack | _____ |
| flip | _____ | dent | _____ |

**Directions:** Now add **-ing** to the same verbs. Double the consonants that should be doubled.

**Like this:**

| | | | |
|---|---|---|---|
| flap | _____flapping_____ | snack | _____snacking_____ |
| scrub | _____ | flip | _____ |
| stock | _____ | rinse | _____ |
| dent | _____ | brag | _____ |
| pet | _____ | lack | _____ |
| rob | _____ | punch | _____ |

5

# Adding The Missing Parts

**Directions:** Make each group of words below into a sentence, adding a subject, a verb, or a subject **and** a verb. Use your imagination! Then write **S** over each subject and **V** over each verb.

**Like this:**

The dishes in the sink

S      V
_____ The dishes in the sink were dirty. _____

1. a leash for your pet

_____

2. dented the table

_____

3. a bowl of punch for the party

_____

4. rinsed the soap out

_____

5. a lack of chairs

_____

6. bragging about his sister

_____

7. the stock on the shelf

_____

8. with a flip of the wrist

_____

Name: _____

# Finding The Mistakes

**Directions:** Circle the four spelling mistakes in each paragraph. Then write the words correctly on the lines below.

According to the newspaper, a man came into the store and stood near a clerk. The clerk was stockking the shelves with watches. Then the man suddenly grabed several watches and raced out of the store. The clerk shouted, "Stop him! He's robing us!" The police searched for the man, but they still lak a suspect.

_____     _____

_____     _____

Tony always braged about the tricks he could do with his skateboard. One day he tried to skate up a ramp and jump over three bikes. Well, he landed on the last bike and dentted it. The last I saw Tony he was runing down the street. The owner of the bike was chasing him and yelling something about punchhing him out.

_____     _____

_____     _____

One day I was peting my dog when I felt something sticky in his fur. It was time for a bath! I put him in a tub of water and scrubed as best I could. Then I rinced the soap out of his fur. He jumped out of the tub, soaking wet, and rolled in some dirt. I sighed and draged him back into the tub. This dog makes me tired sometimes.

_____     _____

_____     _____

Last night my little sister started braging about how fast she could wash the dishes. I told her to prove it. (It was my turn to do the dishes.) She started fliping the dishes around in the sink, washing them as fast as she could. I noticed she was rinseing only about half of them. Finally, it happened. She droped a cup on the floor. Dad made me finish the dishes, but at least she did **some** of them.

_____     _____

_____     _____

7

# Review

**Directions:** Circle the short vowels in the sentence below. (There are two of each short vowel.)

Bob just dropped his bread and butter in wet sand.

**Directions:** Write six sentences using verbs that end with **-ed** or **-ing**. For three sentences, use verbs that need the last consonant doubled. For the other three sentences, use verbs that do not need the last consonant doubled. Here are some verbs you could use: punch, rob, pet, stock, lack, dent, brag, scrub, rinse, flip. Now underline all the nouns in your sentences. Write **S** above the subjects and **V** above the verbs.

                               S        V     V

**Like this:**      My little <u>sister</u> was washing her <u>bike</u>.

                        S        V

                    <u>Mandy</u> picked three <u>people</u> for her <u>team</u>.

1. _____

2. _____

3. _____

4. _____

5. _____

6. _____

**Directions:** Use **pet** as the verb in sentence #1, as the subject in sentence #2, and as a noun (but not the subject) in sentence #3.

**Like this:**
1. A rock <u>dented</u> our car.
2. The <u>dent</u> damaged the side door.
3. I noticed the <u>dent</u> this morning.

1. _____

2. _____

3. _____

Name: _____

# Spelling Words With Long i And Long a

Long **i** is written /ī/. The words in this lesson spell /ī/ two ways: **i-consonant-e** as in h**i**d**e** and **y** as in m**y**. The vowel /ī/ can also be spelled **i** as in k**i**nd and **igh** as in fl**igh**t.

Long **a** is written /ā/. The words in this lesson spell /ā/ **a-consonant-e** as in pl**a**t**e** and **ai** as in p**ai**n. The vowel /ā/ can also be spelled **a** as in **a**ble and **ay** as in d**ay**.

**Directions:** Use words from the word box in these exercises.

| style | bathe | faith | title | dye | pride | daily | praise | spite | scrape |
|---|---|---|---|---|---|---|---|---|---|

1. Write each word in the row that has its vowel sound.

/ī/  _____  _____  _____  _____  _____

/ā/  _____  _____  _____  _____  _____

2. Say the word on the left. Then circle the two other words in that row that have the same vowel sound.

| | | | | |
|---|---|---|---|---|
| faith | date | crack | play | jam |
| spite | high | drill | quilt | sly |
| bathe | bath | social | raid | ape |
| style | clay | twice | while | still |

3. Finish these sentences, using a word with the vowel sound given. Use each word from the word box only once.

The /ī/ _____ of clothes changes every year.

To stay clean, we all need to /ā/ _____ /ā/ _____ .

I liked the book in /ī/ _____ of its /ī/ _____ .

However, the newspaper review did not /ā/ _____ the book.

Why did she /ī/ _____ her hair that color?

Even though we were having problems finishing our project, our teacher said she had /ā/ _____ that we could do it.

Name: _____

# Finding Out About Pronouns

A pronoun is a word that is used in place of a noun. Instead of repeating a noun again and again, we can use a pronoun. Here are some common pronouns:

| I | we | you | he | she | they | it |
|---|----|-----|-----|-----|------|-----|
| me | us | you | him | her | them | it |
| my | our | your | his | her | their | its |

Each pronoun takes the place of a certain noun. If the noun is singular, the pronoun needs to be singular. If the noun is plural, the pronoun should be plural.

**Like this:**   John told **his** parents **he** would be late. The girls said **they** would ride **their** bikes.

**Directions:** In the sentences below draw a line from the noun to the pronoun that takes its place.

**Like this:**   Gail needs the salt. Please pass it to her.

1. The workers had faith they would finish the house in time.

2. Kathy fell and scraped her knees. She put bandaids on them.

3. The teacher told the students he wanted to see their papers.

**Directions:** Cross out some nouns and write the pronoun that could be used.

**Like this:**   Dan needed a book for ~~Dan's~~ his book report.

1. Brian doesn't care about the style of Brian's clothes.

2. Joy dyed Joy's jeans to make the jeans dark blue.

3. Faith said Faith was tired of sharing a bedroom with Faith's two sisters. Faith wanted a room of Faith's own.

4. Bathe babies carefully so the soap doesn't get in the babies' eyes and make the babies cry.

5. When the children held up the children's pictures, we could see the pride in the children's eyes.

Name: _____

# Changing Vowels With A Final e

Adding **e** to the end of some words changes a short vowel to a long vowel.

**Like this:**   mat - mat**e**        sit - sit**e**

**Directions:** Add **e** to the end of these words to make new words.  Then write /ī/ or /ā/ to show the long vowel in the new word. The first one is done for you.

| | | | |
|---|---|---|---|
| mad | made    ā | bit | |
| dim | | tap | |
| hid | | pin | |
| fat | | past | |
| fin | | spit | |
| kit | | bath | |
| win | | rip | |
| hat | | scrap | |
| rid | | twin | |

**Directions:** Answer these questions with words from the word box.

| style | bathe | faith | title | dye | pride | daily | praise | spite | scrape |
|---|---|---|---|---|---|---|---|---|---|

1. Which words are pronounced this way?

/stīl/ _____     /prās/ _____

/skrāp/ _____     /dī/ _____

/prīd/ _____     /spīt/ _____

2. Which word has a **y** that is not pronounced /ī/? _____

# Using Pronouns Correctly

Sometimes people have trouble matching nouns and pronouns. Here is an example: A teacher should always be fair to their students.

Teacher is singular, but their is plural, so they don't match. Still, we can't say "A teacher should always be fair to his students" because teachers are both men and women. "His or her students" sounds awkward.

One easy way to handle this problem is to make teacher plural so it will match their: Teachers should always be fair to their students.

**Directions:** Correct the pronoun problems in these sentences by writing in a different pronoun or by making the noun plural. (If you make the noun plural, make the verb plural, too.) Then draw a line from the noun to its correct pronoun.

**Like this:**     Ron's school won ~~their~~ basketball game.
                                        its

                        cats are
You can tell if ~~a cat is~~ angry by watching their tails.

1. A student should  try to praise their friends' strong points.

2. The group finished their work on time in spite of the deadline.

3. A parent usually has a lot of faith in their children.

4. The company paid their workers once a week.

5. The train made their daily run from Chicago to Detroit.

6. Each student should have a title on their papers.

**Directions:** Finish these sentences by writing in the correct pronouns.

1. Simon fell out of the tree and scraped _____ arm.

2. The citizens felt a deep pride in _____ community.

3. Harry and Sheila wear _____ hair in the same style.

4. I dyed some shirts, but _____ didn't turn out right.

5. The nurse showed the mother how to bathe _____ baby.

6. Our school made $75 from _____ carnival.

Name: _____

# Rhyming And Defining Words

**Directions:** Write the word from the word box that rhymes with each of these. (Some words are not used, and some are used more than once.)

| style | bathe | faith | title | dye | pride | daily | praise | spite | scrape |
|-------|-------|-------|-------|-----|-------|-------|--------|-------|--------|

cape _____    right _____

pile _____    tried _____

gaily _____    pie _____

days _____    dyed _____

dial _____    graze _____

cry _____    write _____

grape _____    fly _____

bite _____    tape _____

tied _____    trays _____

**Directions:** Write the word from the word box that matches each definition.

1. A strong belief: _____

2. A certain way of doing something: _____

3. The name of a book: _____

4. Every day: _____

5. One way to get clean: _____

6. To say what you like about something: _____

7. A feeling of success: _____

8. To change the color: _____

Name: _____

# Writing Poetry

**Directions:** For the first group of poems below, both lines rhyme. Finish each poem, using one of the rhyming words given, another one from page 13, or one you think of yourself.

**Like this:**

mile
pile
dial

Kevin James has a certain style.

<u>To get his way, he'd walk a mile.</u>

ape
grape
cape

Mindy Lou got a very bad scrape!

_____

hide
fried
cried

Sometimes you have to swallow your pride

_____

lays
plays
graze

One dark day I needed some praise

_____

**Directions:** Each poem in this second group has four lines. The second and fourth lines rhyme. Finish these poems with the words given or others.

**Like this:**

cape
tape
grape

Kenny skidded on his bike
And got himself all **scraped**.
Now his bike has a flat tire,
And his whole leg is **taped**.

I
cry
my

I put some water in a bucket
And then threw in some **dye.**

_____

file
dial
Nile

Kelly got her hair cut,
But I don't like the **style**.

_____

ride
hide
cried

When Billy didn't win the race,
It really hurt his **pride**.

_____

Name: _____

# Spelling Possessive Pronouns

A possessive pronoun shows ownership. Pronouns can be possessive, just like nouns. Instead of writing "That is Jill's book," we can write "That is her book" or "That is hers." Instead of "I lost my pencil," we can write "I lost mine." Use these possessive pronouns when you name what is possessed:

my (book)   our (car)   your (hat)   his (leg)   her (hair)   their (group)   its (team)

Use these possessive pronouns when you don't name what is possessed:
mine   ours   yours   his   hers   theirs

Did you notice that possessive pronouns don't use apostrophes?

**Directions:** Finish these sentences by writing in the possesssive pronouns. Make sure you don't use apostrophes.

**Like this:**     This book belongs to Jon.  It is _____his_____ .

1. I brought my lunch.  Did you bring _____ ?

2. I can't do my homework.  I wonder if Nancy figured out _____ .

3. Jason saved his candy bar, but I ate _____ .

4. Our team finished our project, but they didn't finish _____ .

5. They already have their assignment.  When will we get_____ ?

Some people confuse the possessive pronoun **its** with the contraction for **it is**, which is spelled **it's**. The apostrophe in **it's** shows that the **i** in **is** has been left out.

**Directions:** Write **its** or **it's** in each sentence below.

**Like this:**     The book has lost _____its_____ cover.     _____It's_____ going to rain soon.

1. _____ nearly time to go.

2. The horse has hurt _____ leg.

3. Every nation has _____ share of problems.

4. What is _____ name?

5. I think _____ too warm to snow.

6. The teacher said _____ up to us.

Name: _____

# Review

**Directions:** Finish the poems below.  Rhyme the first line with the third line and the second line with the fourth line.

**Like this:**     I know a title for a **book**.
I've known of it for **ages**.
The part that really has me **shook**
Is how to fill the **pages**.

I have a dog I love to **praise**.
His tricks will just amaze **you**.

_____

_____

My favorite jeans were getting **old**
And so I bought some **dye**.

_____

_____

**Directions:** Write sentences for eight of the words in the word box. Include at least one pronoun in each sentence. Draw a line from each pronoun to its noun. (Make sure the pronoun is plural if the noun is plural and remember not to use apostrophes in possessive pronouns.)

| style | bathe | faith | title | dye | pride | daily | praise | spite | scrape |
|-------|-------|-------|-------|-----|-------|-------|--------|-------|--------|

**Like this:**     Pam has faith in <u>her</u> project in spite of <u>its</u> problems.

1. _____

2. _____

3. _____

4. _____

5. _____

Name: _____

# Spelling Words With Long o And Long e

Long **o** is written /ō/. The words in this lesson spell /ō/ two ways: **oa** as in b**oa**t and **o**-consonant-**e** as in h**ope**. This vowel can also be spelled **o** as in **o**pen, **ow** as in gl**ow**, and **ew** as in s**ew**.

Long **e** is written /ē/. The words in this lesson spell /ē/ with **e** as in m**e**, **ee** as in s**ee**n, and **ea** as in pl**ea**se. This vowel can also be spelled **ie** as in bel**ie**ve.

**Directions:** Use words from the word box to complete the exercises.

| release | elect | loan | coax | cheat | screen | vote | decrease | code | goal |

1. Write each word in the row that names at least one of its vowel sounds.

/ō/  _____  _____  _____  _____  _____

/ē/  _____  _____  _____  _____  _____

2. Write the word that is pronounced the way given below.

/skrēn/  _____     /kōd/  _____

/chēt/  _____     /dēkrēs/  _____

/ēlekt/  _____     /vōt/  _____

/rēlēs/  _____     /kōks/  _____

/gōl/  _____     /lōn/  _____

3. Finish these sentences, using a word with the vowel sound given. Use each word from the word box only once.

Can you break the /ō/ _____ so we can read the message?

The jail will /ē/ _____ two prisoners today.

Today we will /ō/ _____ to /ē/ _____ a new mayor.

The /ē/ _____ on the window will help /ē/ _____ the number of flies that come in.

You won't reach your /ō/ _____ if you /ē/ _____ .

Name: _____

# Using Adjectives And Adverbs

Sentences can include nouns, verbs, adjectives, and adverbs. (You know that a noun is the name of a person, place, or thing. A verb is the action word in a sentence, like **eat** and **listen**.)

An adjective is a word or words that describe a noun. Adjectives can tell:
- Which one or what kind — the dog **with floppy ears**, the **lost** child
- How many — **three** wagons, **four** drawers

An adverb is a word or words that tell something about a verb. Adverbs can tell:
- How — ran **quickly**, talked **quietly**
- When — finished **on time**, came **yesterday**
- Where — lived **in an apartment**, drove **to the next town**
- How often — sneezed **twice**, **always** wins

**Directions:** The adjectives and adverbs are underlined in the sentences below. Above each one write **ADJ** for adjective or **ADV** for adverb. Then draw a line to the noun the adjective describes or to the verb the adverb tells about.

                    ⟵——ADJ            ADV⟶        ⟵———— ADV
**Like this:**    A girl in a green jacket quickly released the birds into the sky.

1. A new mayor was elected in our town last week.

2. He carefully put the tall screen between our desks.

3. The new boy in our class moved here from Phoenix.

4. Today the team from our school finally made its first goal.

5. The woman gently coaxed the frightened kitten out of the tree.

**Directions:** Add adjectives and adverbs that answer the questions.

**Like this:**    The boy talked. (Which boy? How?)

    The nervous boy talked loudly.

1. The plant grew. (Which plant? How?)

_____

2. The birds flew. (How many? What kind? Where?)

_____

Name: _____

# Making New Words

**Directions:** Make new words from old ones by adding and subtracting short vowels (/**a**/, /**e**/, /**i**/, /**o**/, and /**u**/), long vowels (/**ī**/, /**ā**/, /**ō**/, and /**ē**/), and consonants. The spelling of some words will change quite a bit with the new vowel. (All of the answers are on page 1, 9, or 17.)

**Like this:**

Pete     -   /ē/   +   /e/  =     _pet_____

1. boat    -   /b/   +   /v/  =  _____

2. kid     -   /i/   +   /ō/  =  _____

3. lean    -   /ē/   +   /ō/  =  _____

4. kicks   -   /i/   +   /ō/  =  _____

5. gull    -   /u/   +   /ō/  =  _____

6. steak   -   /ā/   +   /o/  =  _____

7. line    -   /ī/   +   /ō/  =  _____

8. don't   -   /ō/   +   /e/  =  _____

9. dolly   -   /o/   +   /ā/  =  _____

10. prayed  -   /ā/   +   /ī/  =  _____

11. still   -   /i/   +   /ī/  =  _____

12. lake    -   /ā/   +   /a/  =  _____

13. rents   -   /e/   +   /i/  =  _____

14. rob     -   /o/   +   /ō/  =  _____

15. like    -   /ī/   +   /ā/  =  _____

16. gill    -   /i/   +   /ō/  =  _____

17. lane    -   /ā/   +   /ō/  =  _____

Name: _____

# Recognizing Parts Of Sentences

**Directions:** Write each word or group of words in the column that names how it could be used in a sentence. Several examples are listed for you. Some of the items can be listed in two columns.

| | ADJ | | ADV | |
|---|---|---|---|---|
| **For example:** | a chair <u>behind me</u> | | he was walking <u>behind me</u> | |

| | | | | | |
|---|---|---|---|---|---|
| code | young | slowly | today | finally | screen |
| thirsty | praise | loan | broken | decrease | slowly |
| nearby | twenty | Monday | town | faith | in my hand |
| coax | goal | bathe | release | cheat | down the road |

| Noun | Verb | Adjective | Adverb |
|---|---|---|---|
| _____ | _____ | _____ | _____ |
| _____ | _____ | _____ | _____ |
| _____ | _____ | _____ | _____ |
| _____ | _____ | _____ | _____ |
| _____ | _____ | _____ | _____ |

**Directions:** Now write four sentences, using at least three words from the word box in each one. Mark each word from the word box as a noun (**N**), verb (**V**), adjective (**ADJ**), or adverb (**ADV**).

**Like this:**

    ADJ    ADV          N

Six people slowly counted the votes.

1. _____

2. _____

3. _____

4. _____

Name: _____

# Using Different Forms Of Verbs

To explain what is happening right now, we can use a "plain" verb or we can use **is** or **are** and add **-ing** to the verb.

**Like this:**  We eat.  We **are** eat**ing**.

Remember that when a verb already ends with **e**, drop the **e** before adding another ending.

**Like this:**  He serves.  He **is** serv**ing**.

**Directions:** Finish each sentence with the correct form of the verb, telling what is happening right now. Read carefully, as some sentences already have **is** or **are**.

**Like this:**  Scott is (loan) _____loaning_____ Jenny his math book.

Jenny (like) _____likes_____ reading better than math.

1. The court is (release) _____ the prisoner early.

2. Jack and Jill (write) _____ their notes in code.

3. Are you (vote) _____ for Henry?

4. The girls are (coax) _____ the dog into the bathtub.

5. This nation (elect) _____ a president every four years.

6. My little brother (cheat) _____ when we play Monopoly.

7. Is she (hide) _____ behind the screen?

To explain what already happened, we can add **-ed** to many verbs or we can use **was** or **were** and add **-ing** to the verb.

**Like this:**  I watch**ed**. I **was** watch**ing**.

**Directions:** As you did above, write in the correct forms of the verbs. This time, tell what already happened.

**Like this:**  We (walk) ___walked___ there yesterday. They were (talk) ___talking___.

8. The government was (decrease) _____ our taxes.

9. Was anyone (cheat) _____ in this game?

10. We were (try) _____ to set goals for the project.

# Being Specific

Our writing is clearer and more interesting when we use "German shepherd" instead of "dog" and when we write "lemon pie" instead of "dessert." Specific words tell readers what we really mean.

**Directions:** Write a more specific word or words for each general one. The first one is done for you.

| | | | |
|---|---|---|---|
| store | _K-Mart_ | building | _____ |
| game | _____ | TV show | _____ |
| pet | _____ | worker | _____ |
| car | _____ | dessert | _____ |
| bird | _____ | clothing | _____ |

**Directions:** Rewrite these sentences, using more specific words and adding adjectives and adverbs so the reader knows exactly what you mean. Mark at least one adjective (ADJ) and one adverb (ADV) in each of your sentences.

                                    ADJ          ADJ                                    ADV      ADV
**Like this:** The tree fell down.  The ancient oak in our front yard was knocked down by high winds.

1. The road led to a town.

_____

2. The girl heard a sound.

_____

3. The boy finished his project.

_____

4. The flower was pretty.

_____

5. The baby made a mess.

_____

6. Pat rode her new bike.

_____

# Finishing A Crossword Puzzle

**Directions:** Write the word to match each definition in the spaces that start with the same number. (If you are having trouble spelling the words, they are in the word box on page 17.)

**Across**
2. Not to follow the rules
4. To let something go
6. The front of a television
8. To take part in an election
9. To lend someone something
10. To beg

**Down**
1. To make something smaller
3. Symbols
5. Something you want to reach
7. To select someone for a certain position

# Review

**Directions:** Pretend your school is going to vote on new school colors. The grade four class wants one set of colors, maybe blue and gold, but your class wants different colors. Follow these steps to write a story about this election:

**Step One:** On another sheet of paper, write your ideas about what might happen. How could your class convince other classes to vote for the colors you want? What might the grade four class do to get students to vote for their colors?

**Step Two:** Look over your ideas and pick those you want to use in your story. Put them in order so your story has a beginning (explaining the situation), a middle (telling what everyone did), and an end (showing how the election turned out and how everyone felt about it).

**Step Three:** Write your story in sentences.

**A.** Include at least six of these words: release, elect, loan, coax, cheat, screen, vote, decrease, code, goal.

**B.** Use adjectives and adverbs to help explain what happens.

**C.** Use specific words instead of general ones.

**D.** Use both "plain" verbs and the **-ing** forms (with **is, are, was,** or **were**).

**Step Four:** Read your story out loud to a partner and listen while your partner reads his or hers. Are both stories clear? Did either of you leave anything out? Did you use specific words?

**Step Five:** Make any needed changes and rewrite your story below. Give it a  title. Use more paper if you need it. Maybe your teacher will post the stories on the wall or bulletin board so youcan read each others' and find out what happened in all the elections.

_____

_____

_____

_____

_____

_____

_____

Name: _____

# Spelling Words With Digraphs

A digraph is two consonant letters pronounced as one consonant sound. Here are three digraphs: /**sh**/ as in **sh**ell, /**ch**/ as in **ch**ew, and /**th**/ as in **th**in.

**Directions:** Write in **sh**, **ch**, or **th** to complete each word below.

1. __ __ reaten

2. __ __ ill

3. __ __ ock

4. __ __ iver

5. __ __ aw

6. __ __ allenge

7. peri __ __

8. __ __ ield

9. __ __ art

10. __ __ rive

**Directions:** Finish these sentences with a word that contains the digraph given.

1. A trip to the South Pole would really be a /ch/_____ .

2. The ice there never /th/ _____ because the temperature averages -50 C.

3. How can any living thing /th/ _____ or even live when it's so cold?

4. With six months of total darkness and those icy temperatures, any plants would soon /sh/

_____ .

5. Even the thought of that numbing cold makes me /sh/ _____ .

6. The cold and darkness /th/ _____ the lives of explorers.

7. The explorers take along maps and /ch/ _____ to help them findtheir way.

8. Special clothing helps protect and /sh/ _____ them from the cold.

9. Still, the weather must be a /sh/ _____ at first.

10. Did someone leave a door open? Suddenly I feel a /ch/ _____ .

25

# Choosing "Joining Words"

Too many short sentences make writing seem choppy, but we can combine some of these sentences with "joining words."

**Directions:** Use one of the "joining words" given to combine each pair of sentences.

**Like this:**

or
but
before

I was wearing my winter coat. I started to shiver.

_I was wearing my winter coat, but I started to shiver._

when
but
and

1. Animals all need water. They may perish without it.

_____

after
or
but

2. The sun came out. The ice began to thaw.

_____

and
but
because

3. The sun came out. The day was still chilly.

_____

but
when
or

4. Will the flowers perish? Will they thrive?

_____

or
when
but

5. The bear came closer. We began to feel threatened.

_____

but
because
before

6. Winning was a challenge. Our team didn't have much experience.

_____

but
because
before

7. Winning was a challenge. Our team was up to it.

_____

**Directions:** Write three sentences of your own. Use one of these joining words in each sentence: **and, but, or, when, after, because, so, before.**

_____

_____

_____

Name: _____

# Cracking The Code

**Directions:** Each symbol below stands for a consonant letter. Write the letters on the lines under each symbol. Then add vowels to spell words from the word box.

| challenge | shock | thaw | chart | threaten | perish | chill | shiver | thrive | shield |
|-----------|-------|------|-------|----------|--------|-------|--------|--------|--------|

| ☆ | + | ○ | X | Σ | □ | ◇ | △ | § | # | ∅ | π | = |
|---|---|---|---|---|---|---|---|---|---|---|---|---|
| c | d | g | h | k | l | n | p | r | s | t | v | w |

**Like this:**

|  | # | X | ☆ | Σ |
|--|---|---|---|---|
|  | s | h | c | k |

shock

1. ∅  X  =

2. ☆  X  □  □

3. #  X  π  §

4. △  §  #  X

5. #  X  □  +

6. ☆  X  §  ∅

7. ∅  X  §  π

8. ∅  X  §  ∅  ◇

9. ☆  X  □  □  ◇  ○

# Combining Ideas

When two sentences repeat some of the same information, we often can combine them into one sentence with fewer words.

**Directions:** Combine each set of sentences into one sentence. Some will have two subjects, some will have two verbs, and some will be joined with words such as **when, before, but**, or **because**.

**Like this:**     The sun came out. The river started to thaw. The pond also thawed.

_____ When the sun came out, the river and pond started to thaw.

1. The rain continued for days. The river flooded. The river threatened to cover the roads.

_____

_____

2. The catcher shivered in the cold morning air. The batter shivered, too. They had forgotten their jackets.

_____

_____

3. I talked to my plants. I watered them every day. They still died.

_____

_____

4. Germs thrive on dirty hands. Bacteria thrive, too. They both multiply there.

_____

_____

**Directions:** Write your own sentences, following the instructions.

1. Write a sentence with two subjects:

_____

2. Write a sentence with two verbs:

_____

3. Write a sentence with two subjects and two verbs:

_____

Name: _____

# Searching For Synonyms

**Directions:** Circle a word or a phrase in each sentence that is a synonym for a word in the word box. Write the synonym from the word box on the line.

| challenge   shock   thaw   chart   threaten   perish   chill   shiver   thrive   shield |

**Like this:**     The writing was in an (old) code.    _ancient_____

1. A fish out of water will quickly die.          _____

2. The ice carving is beginning to melt.          _____

3. I was amazed when I saw how he looked.      _____

4. The puppy was trembling with excitement.     _____

5. Ferns need moisture to grow well.             _____

6. Are you trying to scare me?                   _____

7. Let the salad get cold in the refrigerator.    _____

8. She tried to protect him from the truth.       _____

9. He made a list of different kinds of birds.    _____

10. They dared us to enter the contest.          _____

**Directions:** Write your own sentences for five words from the word box to prove you know what they mean.  (If you're not sure, look them up in a dictionary.) Trade your sentences with someone else. Do you think that person understands the words he or she used in sentences?

_____

_____

_____

_____

_____

Name: _____

# Knowing When To Stop

Although we can combine some of our short sentences, we also need to know when to end a sentence and start a new one.

**Directions:** Use periods, question marks, and exclamation marks to show where sentences should end in these paragraphs. Circle the first letter in the first word of each new sentence to show it should be a capital letter.

(t)he farmers were worried about their orange crop. temperatures that night were supposed to reach a record low the chill might stop the buds on the trees from developing into oranges the drop in temperature threatened  to ruin the entire year's crop

on our last camping trip I was really glad to have my new sleeping bag the other campers were shivering in their sleeping bags, but mine had a special lining that shielded me from the cold the next morning I noticed  ice on a puddle starting to thaw I was shocked it really had been cold that night thank goodness for my new sleeping  bag

**Directions:** Some of the periods in the paragraphs below are in the wrong place. Rewrite each paragraph, putting periods where they belong and combining some of the shorter sentences.

The Antarctic Circle. Is the area around the South Pole. Days there are six months long. Nights are also six months long. When it is day at the South Pole. It is night at the North Pole.

_____

_____

Some people think tourists should not go into the Antarctic Circle. Because they disturb the animals that live there. Tours tend to take place. At the same time the penguins begin their breeding season. The seals also breed then. Sometimes the animals leave the breeding areas. When they feel threatened by tourists. They also are scared of the tourists' helicopters.

_____

_____

_____

# ANSWER KEY

*This Answer Key has been designed so that it may be easily removed if you so desire.*

## MASTER SPELLING/WRITING
## 5

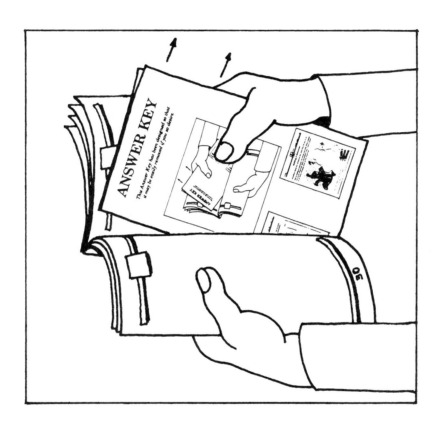

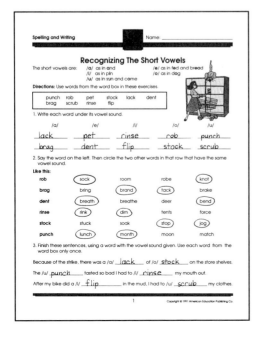

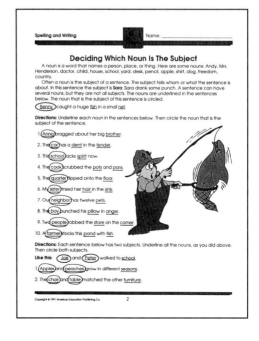

## Using Math On Words

**Directions:** Add and subtract sounds to make new words. The spelling of the whole word may change.

**Like this:**

stock - /o/ + /i/ = __stick__

1. punch - /u/ + /i/ = __pinch__
2. lack + /b/ = __black__
3. flip - /i/ + /a/ = __flap__
4. rob - /o/ + /i/ = __rib__
5. lack + /i/ = __lick__
6. scrub - /k/ + /h/ = __shrub__
7. pet - /e/ + /a/ = __pat__
8. scrub - /sk/ = __rub__
9. flip - /fl/ + /gr/ = __grip__
10. lack - /a/ + /u/ = __luck__
11. rinse + /p/ = __prince__
12. net - /e/ + /u/ = __nut__
13. rob - /o/ + /u/ = __rub__
14. brag - /b/ + /d/ = __drag__
15. flip - /i/ + /a/ = __flap__
16. scrub - /ru/ + /a/ = __scab__
17. lack - /a/ + /o/ = __lock__
18. stock - /o/ + /u/ = __stuck__

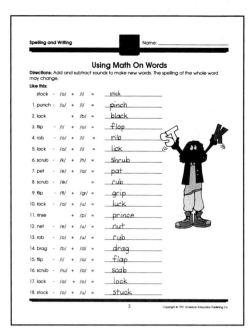

---

## Finding Subjects And Verbs

A verb is the action word in a sentence. It tells what the subject does (for example: **build, live, express, fasten**) or that it exists (**is, are, was, were,** and others). Remember that a verb can be two or more words: **is walking, are listening, was writing, were learning.**

**Directions:** Underline the subject and verb in each sentence below. Write **S** over the subject and **V** over the verb. If the verb is two words, mark them both.

**Like this:** Dennis was drinking some punch.　　The punch was too sweet.

1. Hayley brags about her dog all the time.
2. Mrs. Thomas scrubbed the dirt off her car.
3. Then her son rinsed the soap off.
4. The teacher was flipping through the cards.
5. Jenny's rabbit was hungry and thirsty.
6. Your science report lacks a title.
7. Mike and Chris are stocking the shelves with cans of soup.
8. The accident caused a huge dent in our car.

Just as sentences can have two subjects, they can have two verbs.

**Like this:** Jennifer fed her dog and gave him clean water.

**Directions:** Underline all the subjects and verbs in these sentences. Write **S** over the subjects and **V** over the verbs.

1. The worker scrubbed and rinsed the floor.
2. The men came and stocked the lake with fish.
3. Someone broke a window and robbed the store.
4. Carrie punched a hole in the paper and threaded yarn through the hole.
5. Julie and Pat turned their bikes around and went home.

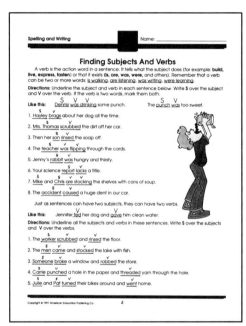

---

## Knowing When To Double Consonants

Many people aren't sure whether to double the last consonant of verbs when they add endings such as **-ing** and **-ed**. Is it **riped** or **ripped**? Here is the rule: Double the last consonant of verbs that have short vowel sounds (like all the verbs in the word box on page 1) and end with only one consonant letter (like **some** of them).

Thus, **rip** becomes **ripped** and **beg** becomes **begging**. However, we don't double the last consonant in **rock.** Even though it has a short vowel, it ends with two consonant letters: **ck.** So **rock** becomes **rocked.**

**Directions:** Add **-ed** to the verbs below. Be careful about which last consonants you double. Remember that when a verb ends with **e,** drop the **e** before adding an ending (taste, tasted, tasting).

**Like this:**

| | | | |
|---|---|---|---|
| top | __topped__ | rip | __ripped__ |
| pet | __petted__ | punch | __punched__ |
| rob | __robbed__ | rinse | __rinsed__ |
| brag | __bragged__ | stock | __stocked__ |
| scrub | __scrubbed__ | lack | __lacked__ |
| flip | __flipped__ | dent | __dented__ |

**Directions:** Now add **-ing** to the same verbs. Double the consonants that should be doubled.

**Like this:**

| | | | |
|---|---|---|---|
| flap | __flapping__ | snack | __snacking__ |
| scrub | __scrubbing__ | flip | __flipping__ |
| stock | __stocking__ | rinse | __rinsing__ |
| dent | __denting__ | brag | __bragging__ |
| pet | __petting__ | lack | __lacking__ |
| rob | __robbing__ | punch | __punching__ |

---

## Adding The Missing Parts

**Directions:** Make each group of words below into a sentence, adding a subject, a verb, or a subject **and** a verb. Use your imagination! Then write **S** over each subject and **V** over each verb.

**Like this:**

The dishes in the sink
__The dishes in the sink were dirty__

1. a leash for your pet
__sentences will vary__

2. dented the table
_____

3. a bowl of punch for the party
_____

4. rinsed the soap out
_____

5. a lack of chairs
_____

6. bragging about his sister
_____

7. the stock on the shelf
_____

8. with a flip of the wrist
_____

---

## Finding The Mistakes

**Directions:** Circle the four spelling mistakes in each paragraph. Then write the words correctly on the lines below.

According to the newspaper, a man came into the store and stood near a clerk. The clerk was stockking the shelves with watches. Then the man suddenly grabed several watches and raced out of the store. The clerk shouted, "Stop him! He's robing us!" The police searched for the man, but they still lak a suspect.

| | |
|---|---|
| __stocking__ | __grabbed__ |
| __robbing__ | __lack__ |

Tony always braged about the tricks he could do with his skateboard. One day he tried to skate up a ramp and jump over three bikes. Well, he landed on the last bike and dentted it. The last I saw Tony he was runing down the street. The owner of the bike was chasing him and yelling something about punchhing him out.

| | |
|---|---|
| __bragged__ | __dented__ |
| __running__ | __punching__ |

One day I was peting my dog when I felt something sticky in his fur. It was time for a bath! I put him in a tub of water and scrubed as best I could. Then I rinced the soap out of his fur. He jumped out of the tub, soaking wet, and rolled in some dirt. I sighed and draged him back into the tub. This dog makes me tired sometimes.

| | |
|---|---|
| __petting__ | __scrubbed__ |
| __rinsed__ | __dragged__ |

Last night my little sister started braging about how fast she could wash the dishes. I told her to prove it. (It was my turn to do the dishes.) She started fliping the dishes around in the sink, washing them as fast as she could. I noticed she was rinseing only about half of them. Finally, it happened. She droped a cup on the floor. Dad made me finish the dishes, but at least she did **some** of them.

| | |
|---|---|
| __bragging__ | __flipping__ |
| __rinsing__ | __dropped__ |

---

## Review

**Directions:** Circle the short vowels in the sentence below. (There are two of each short vowel.)

Bob just dropped his bread and butter in wet sand.

**Directions:** Write six sentences using verbs that end with **-ed** or **-ing.** For three sentences, use verbs that need the last consonant doubled. For the other three sentences, use verbs that do not need the last consonant doubled. Here are some verbs you could use: punch, rob, pet, stock, lack, dent, brag, scrub, rinse, flip. Now underline all the nouns in your sentences. Write **S** above the subjects and **V** above the verbs.

**Like this:** My little sister was washing her bike.
Mandy picked three people for her team.

1. __Sentences will vary__
2. _____
3. _____
4. _____
5. _____
6. _____

**Directions:** Use **pet** as the verb in sentence #1, as the subject in sentence #2, and as a noun (but not the subject) in sentence #3.

**Like this:**
1. A rock dented our car.
2. The dent damaged the side door.
3. I noticed the dent this morning.

1. __Sentences will vary__
2. _____
3. _____

## Spelling Words With Long i And Long a

Long i is written /ĭ/. The words in this lesson spell /ĭ/ two ways: i-consonant-e as in hide and y as in my. The vowel /ĭ/ can also be spelled i as in kind and igh as in flight.

Long a is written /ā/. The words in this lesson spell /ā/ a-consonant-e as in plate and ai as in pain. The vowel /ā/ can also be spelled a as in able and ay as in day.

**Directions:** Use words from the word box in these exercises.

| style | bathe | faith | title | dye | pride | daily | praise | spite | scrape |

1. Write each word in the row that has its vowel sound.

/ĭ/　　style　　title　　dye　　pride　　spite

/ā/　　bathe　　faith　　daily　　praise　　scrape

2. Say the word on the left. Then circle the two other words in that row that have the same vowel sound.

| faith | (date) | crack | (play) | jam |
| spite | (high) | drill | quit | (sly) |
| bathe | bath | social | (raid) | (ape) |
| style | clay | (twice) | (while) | still |

3. Finish these sentences, using a word with the vowel sound given. Use each word from the word box only once.

The /ĭ/ __style__ of clothes changes every year.

To stay clean, we all need to /ā/ __bathe__ /ā/ __daily__

I liked the book in /ĭ/ __spite__ of its /ĭ/ __title__

However, the newspaper review did not /ā/ __praise__ the book.

Why did she /ĭ/ __dye__ her hair that color?

Even though we were having problems finishing our project, our teacher said she had /ā/ __faith__ that we could do it.

---

## Finding Out About Pronouns

A pronoun is a word that is used in place of a noun. Instead of repeating a noun again and again, we can use a pronoun. Here are some common pronouns:

| I | we | you | he | she | they | it |
| me | us | you | him | her | them | it |
| my | our | your | his | her | their | its |

Each pronoun takes the place of a certain noun. If the noun is singular, the pronoun needs to be singular. If the noun is plural, the pronoun should be plural.

**Like this:** John told his parents he would be late. The girls said they would ride their bikes.

**Directions:** In the sentences below draw a line from the noun to the pronoun that takes its place.

**Like this:** Gail needs the salt. Please pass it to her.

1. The workers had faith they would finish the house in time.

2. Kathy fell and scraped her knees. She put bandaids on them.

3. The teacher told the students he wanted to see their papers.

**Directions:** Cross out some nouns and write the pronoun that could be used.

**Like this:** Dan needed a book for Dan's book report.　his

1. Brian doesn't care about the style of Brian's clothes.　his

2. Joy dyed Joy's jeans to make the jeans dark blue.　her　them

3. Faith said Faith was tired of sharing a bedroom with Faith's two sisters. Faith wanted a room of Faith's own.　she　her　She　her

4. Bathe babies carefully so the soap doesn't get in the babies' eyes and make the babies cry.　their　them

5. When the children held up the children's pictures, we could see the pride in the children's eyes.　their　their

---

## Changing Vowels With A Final e

Adding e to the end of some words changes a short vowel to a long vowel.

**Like this:** mat - mate　sit - site

**Directions:** Add e to the end of these words to make new words. Then write /ĭ/ or /ā/ to show the long vowel in the new word. The first one is done for you.

| mad | made ā | bit | bite ī |
| dim | dime ī | tap | tape ā |
| hid | hide ī | pin | pine ī |
| fat | fate ā | past | paste ā |
| fin | fine ī | spit | spite ī |
| kit | kite ī | bath | bathe ā |
| win | wine ī | rip | ripe ī |
| hat | hate ā | scrap | scrape ā |
| rid | ride ī | twin | twine ī |

**Directions:** Answer these questions with words from the word box.

| style | bathe | faith | title | dye | pride | daily | praise | spite | scrape |

1. Which words are pronounced this way?

/stĭl/ __style__　　/prās/ __praise__

/skrāp/ __scrape__　　/dĭ/ __dye__

/prĭd/ __pride__　　/spĭt/ __spite__

2. Which word has a y that is not pronounced /ĭ/? __daily__

---

## Using Pronouns Correctly

Sometimes people have trouble matching nouns and pronouns. Here is an example:
A teacher should always be fair to their students.

Teacher is singular, but their is plural, so they don't match. Still, we can't say "A teacher should always be fair to his students" because teachers are both men and women. "His or her students" sounds awkward.

One easy way to handle this problem is to make teacher plural so it will match their: Teachers should always be fair to their students.

**Directions:** Correct the pronoun problems in these sentences by writing in a different pronoun or by making the noun plural. (If you make the noun plural, make the verb plural, too.) Then draw a line from the noun to its correct pronoun.

**Like this:** Ron's school won their basketball game.　its
You can tell if a cat is angry by watching their tails.　cats are

1. A student should try to praise their friends' strong points.　his/her

2. The group finished their work on time in spite of the deadline.　its

3. A parent usually has a lot of faith in their children.　Parents　have

4. The company paid their workers once a week.　its

5. The train made their daily run from Chicago to Detroit.　its

6. Each student should have a title on their papers.　his/her

**Directions:** Finish these sentences by writing in the correct pronouns.

1. Simon fell out of the tree and scraped __his__ arm.

2. The citizens felt a deep pride in __their__ community.

3. Harry and Sheila wear __their__ hair in the same style.

4. I dyed some shirts, but __they__ didn't turn out right.

5. The nurse showed the mother how to bathe __her__ baby.

6. Our school made $75 from __its__ carnival.

---

## Rhyming And Defining Words

**Directions:** Write the word from the word box that rhymes with each of these. (Some words are not used, and some are used more than once.)

| style | bathe | faith | title | dye | pride | daily | praise | spite | scrape |

| cape | scrape | right | spite |
| pile | style | tried | pride |
| gaily | daily | pie | dye |
| days | praise | dyed | pride |
| dial | style | graze | praise |
| cry | dye | write | spite |
| grape | scrape | fly | dye |
| bite | spite | tape | scrape |
| tied | pride | trays | praise |

**Directions:** Write the word from the word box that matches each definition.

1. A strong belief: __faith__

2. A certain way of doing something: __style__

3. The name of a book: __title__

4. Every day: __daily__

5. One way to get clean: __bathe__

6. To say what you like about something: __praise__

7. A feeling of success: __pride__

8. To change the color: __dye__

---

## Writing Poetry

**Directions:** For the first group of poems below, both lines rhyme. Finish each poem, using one of the rhyming words given, another one from page 13, or one you think of yourself.

**Like this:**

mile　　Kevin James has a certain style.
pile　　__To get his way, he'd walk a mile__
dial

ape　　Mindy Lou got a very bad scrape!
grape　　__poem completions will vary__
cape

hide　　Sometimes you have to swallow your pride.
fried
cried

lays　　One dark day I needed some praise
plays
graze

**Directions:** Each poem in this second group has four lines. The second and fourth lines rhyme. Finish these poems with the words given or others.

**Like this:**

cape　　Kenny skidded on his bike
tape　　And got himself all scraped.
grape　　Now his bike has a flat tire.
　　　　And his whole leg is taped.

I　　I put some water in a bucket
cry　　And then threw in some dye.
my　　__poem completions will vary__

file　　Kelly got her hair cut.
dial　　But I don't like the style.
Nile

ride　　When Billy didn't win the race,
hide　　It really hurt his pride.
cried

## Spelling Possessive Pronouns

A possessive pronoun shows ownership. Pronouns can be possessive, just like nouns. Instead of writing "That is Jill's book," we can write "That is her book" or "That is hers." Instead of "I lost my pencil," we can write "I lost mine." Use these possessive pronouns when you name what is possessed:

   my (book)   our (car)   your (hat)   his (leg)   her (hair)   their (group)   its (team)

Use these possessive pronouns when you don't name what is possessed:

   mine   ours   yours   his   hers   theirs

Did you notice that possessive pronouns don't use apostrophes?

**Directions:** Finish these sentences by writing in the possessive pronouns. Make sure you don't use apostrophes.

Like this:    This book belongs to Jon. It is ___his___ .

1. I brought my lunch. Did you bring __yours__ ?

2. I can't do my homework. I wonder if Nancy figured out __hers__

3. Jason saved his candy bar, but I ate __mine__ .

4. Our team finished our project, but they didn't finish __theirs__ .

5. They already have their assignment. When will we get __ours__ ?

Some people confuse the possessive pronoun **its** with the contraction for **it is**, which is spelled **it's**. The apostrophe in **it's** shows that the **i** in **is** has been left out.

**Directions:** Write **its** or **it's** in each sentence below.

Like this:    The book has lost __its__ cover. __It's__ going to rain soon.

1. __It's__ nearly time to go.

2. The horse has hurt __its__ leg.

3. Every nation has __its__ share of problems.

4. What is __its__ name?

5. I think __it's__ too warm to snow.

6. The teacher said __it's__ up to us.

---

## Using Adjectives And Adverbs

Sentences can include nouns, verbs, adjectives, and adverbs. (You know that a noun is the name of a person, place, or thing. A verb is the action word in a sentence, like **eat** and **listen**.)

An adjective is a word or words that describe a noun. Adjectives can tell:
- Which one or what kind — the dog **with floppy ears**, the **lost** child
- How many — **three** wagons, **four** drawers

An adverb is a word or words that tell something about a verb. Adverbs can tell:
- How — ran **quickly**, talked **quietly**
- When — finished **on time**, came **yesterday**
- Where — lived **in an apartment**, drove **to the next town**
- How often — sneezed **twice**, **always** wins

**Directions:** The adjectives and adverbs are underlined in the sentences below. Above each one write **ADJ** for adjective or **ADV** for adverb. Then draw a line to the noun the adjective describes or to the verb the adverb tells about.

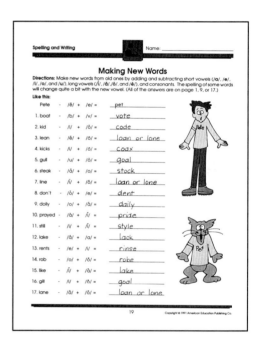

Like this:    A girl in a green jacket quickly released the birds into the sky.

1. A new mayor was elected in our town last week.
2. He carefully put the tall screen between our desks.
3. The new boy in our class moved here from Phoenix.
4. Today the team from our school finally made its first goal.
5. The woman gently coaxed the frightened kitten out of the tree.

**Directions:** Add adjectives and adverbs that answer the questions.

Like this:    The boy talked. (Which boy? How?)

    The nervous boy talked loudly.

1. The plant grew. (Which plant? How?)

     _sentences will vary_

2. The birds flew. (How many? What kind? Where?)

     _____

---

## Review

**Directions:** Finish the poems below. Rhyme the first line with the third line and the second line with the fourth line.

Like this:    I know a title for a **book**.
     I've known of it for **ages**.
     The part that really has me **shook**
     Is how to fill the **pages**.

I have a dog I love to **praise**.
His tricks will just amaze **you**.

     _poem completions will vary_

My favorite jeans were getting **old**
And so I bought some **dye**.

     _____
     _____

**Directions:** Write sentences for eight of the words in the word box. Include at least one pronoun in each sentence. Draw a line from each pronoun to its noun. (Make sure the pronoun is plural if the noun is plural and remember not to use apostrophes in possessive pronouns.)

| style | bathe | faith | title | dye | pride | daily | praise | spite | scrape |
|---|---|---|---|---|---|---|---|---|---|

Like this:    Pam has faith in her project in spite of its problems.

1. _sentences will vary_

2. _____

3. _____

4. _____

5. _____

---

## Making New Words

**Directions:** Make new words from old ones by adding and subtracting short vowels (/a/, /e/, /i/, /o/, and /u/), long vowels (/ā/, /ē/, /ī/, /ō/, and /ū/), and consonants. The spelling of some words will change quite a bit with the new vowel. (All of the answers are on page 1, 9, or 17.)

Like this:

   Pete   -   /ē/ + /e/ =   _pet_

1. boat   -   /ō/ + /v/ =   _vote_

2. kid   -   /i/ + /ō/ =   _code_

3. lean   -   /ē/ + /ō/ =   _loan or lone_

4. kicks   -   /i/ + /ō/ =   _coax_

5. gull   -   /u/ + /ō/ =   _goal_

6. steak   -   /ā/ + /o/ =   _stock_

7. line   -   /ī/ + /ō/ =   _loan or lone_

8. don't   -   /ō/ + /e/ =   _dent_

9. dolly   -   /o/ + /ā/ =   _daily_

10. prayed   -   /ā/ + /ī/ =   _pride_

11. still   -   /i/ + /ī/ =   _style_

12. lake   -   /ā/ + /a/ =   _lack_

13. rents   -   /e/ + /i/ =   _rinse_

14. rob   -   /o/ + /ō/ =   _robe_

15. like   -   /ī/ + /ā/ =   _lake_

16. gill   -   /i/ + /ō/ =   _goal_

17. lane   -   /ā/ + /ō/ =   _loan or lone_

---

## Spelling Words With Long o And Long e

Long **o** is written /ō/. The words in this lesson spell /ō/ two ways: **oa** as in **boat** and **o-consonant-e** as in **hope**. This vowel can also be spelled **o** as in **open**, **ow** as in **glow**, and **ew** as in **sew**.

Long **e** is written /ē/. The words in this lesson spell /ē/ with **e** as in **me**, **ee** as in **seen**, and **ea** as in **please**. This vowel can also be spelled **ie** as in **believe**.

**Directions:** Use words from the word box to complete the exercises.

| release | elect | loan | coax | cheat | screen | decrease | code | goal |
|---|---|---|---|---|---|---|---|---|

1. Write each word in the row that names at least one of its vowel sounds.

/ō/    _loan_    _coax_    _vote_    _code_    _goal_

/ē/    _release_    _elect_    _screen_    _decrease_    _cheat_

2. Write the word that is pronounced the way given below.

/skrēn/   _screen_     /kōd/   _code_

/chēt/   _cheat_     /dēkrēs/   _decrease_

/ēlekt/   _elect_     /vōt/   _vote_

/rēlēs/   _release_     /kōks/   _coax_

/gōl/   _goal_     /lōn/   _loan_

3. Finish these sentences, using a word with the vowel sound given. Use each word from the word box only once.

Can you break the /ō/ _code_ so we can read the message?

The jail will /ē/ _release_ two prisoners today.

Today we will /ō/ _vote_ to /ē/ _elect_ a new mayor.

The /ē/ _screen_ on the window will help /ē/ _decrease_ the number of flies that come in.

You won't reach your /ō/ _goal_ if you /ē/ _cheat_ .

---

## Recognizing Parts Of Sentences

**Directions:** Write each word or group of words in the column that names how it could be used in a sentence. Several examples are listed for you. Some of the items can be listed in two columns.

For example:    a chair behind me (ADJ)    he was walking behind me (ADV)

| code | young | slowly | today | finally | screen |
|---|---|---|---|---|---|
| thirsty | praise | loan | broken | decrease | slowly |
| nearby | twenty | Monday | town | faith | in my hand |
| coax | goal | bathe | release | cheat | down the road |

| Noun | Verb | Adjective | Adverb |
|---|---|---|---|
| vote | vote | behind me | behind me |
| loan | elect | six | in the morning |
| decrease | loan | broken | quietly |
| Monday | decrease | twenty | slowly |
| town | coax | young | nearby |
| faith | bathe | thirsty | Monday |

**Directions:** Now write four sentences, using at least three words from the word box in each one. Mark each word from the word box as a noun (**N**), verb (**V**), adjective (**ADJ**), or adverb (**ADV**).

Like this:    Six people slowly counted the votes. (ADJ ADV N)

1. _sentences will vary_

2. _____

3. _____

4. _____

## Using Different Forms Of Verbs

To explain what is happening right now, we can use a "plain" verb and we can use **is** or **are** and add **-ing** to the verb.

**Like this:**    We eat.   We **are** eat**ing**.

Remember that when a verb already ends with **e**, drop the **e** before adding another ending.

**Like this:**    He serves.   He **is** serv**ing**.

**Directions:** Finish each sentence with the correct form of the verb, telling what is happening right now. Read carefully, as some sentences already have **is** or **are**.

**Like this:**   Scott is (loan) ___loaning___ Jenny his math book.

     Jenny (like) ___likes___ reading better than math.

1. The court is (release) ___releasing___ the prisoner early.

2. Jack and Jill (write) ___write___ their notes in code.

3. Are you (vote) ___voting___ for Henry?

4. The girls are (coax) ___coaxing___ the dog into the bathtub.

5. This nation (elect) ___elects___ a president every four years.

6. My little brother (cheat) ___cheats___ when we play Monopoly.

7. Is she (hide) ___hiding___ behind the screen?

To explain what already happened, we can add **-ed** to many verbs or we can use **was** or **were** and add **-ing** to the verb.

**Like this:**   I watched.   I **was** watch**ing**.

**Directions:** As you did above, write in the correct forms of the verbs. This time, tell what already happened.

**Like this:**   We (walk) ___walked___ there yesterday. They were (talk) ___talking___.

8. The government was (decrease) ___decreasing___ our taxes.

9. Was anyone (cheat) ___cheating___ in this game?

10. We were (try) ___trying___ to set goals for the project.

21    Copyright © 1991 American Education Publishing Co.

---

## Being Specific

Our writing is clearer and more interesting when we use "German shepherd" instead of "dog" and when we write "lemon pie" instead of "dessert." Specific words tell readers what we really mean.

**Directions:** Write a more specific word or words for each general one. The first one is done for you.

| | | | |
|---|---|---|---|
| store | K-Mart | building | |
| game | responses will vary | TV show | |
| pet | | worker | |
| car | | dessert | |
| bird | | clothing | |

**Directions:** Rewrite these sentences, using more specific words and adding adjectives and adverbs so the reader knows exactly what you mean. Mark at least one adjective (ADJ) and one adverb (ADV) in each of your sentences.

       ADJ     ADJ        ADV     ADV

**Like this:** The tree fell down. The ancient oak in our front yard was knocked down by high winds.

1. The road led to a town.    Sentences will vary

2. The girl heard a sound.

3. The boy finished his project.

4. The flower was pretty.

5. The baby made a mess.

6. Pat rode her new bike.

Copyright © 1991 American Education Publishing Co.    22

---

## Finishing A Crossword Puzzle

**Directions:** Write the word to match each definition in the spaces that start with the same number. (If you are having trouble spelling the words, they are in the word box on page 17.)

**Across**
2. Not to follow the rules
4. To let something go
6. The front of a television
8. To take part in an election
9. To lend someone something
10. To beg

**Down**
1. To make something smaller
3. Symbols
5. Something you want to reach
7. To select someone for a certain position

23

---

## Review

**Directions:** Pretend your school is going to vote on new school colors. The grade four class wants one set of colors, maybe blue and gold, but your class wants different colors. Follow these steps to write a story about this election:

**Step One:** On another sheet of paper, write your ideas about what might happen. How could your class convince other classes to vote for the colors you want? What might the grade four class do to get students to vote for their colors?

**Step Two:** Look over your ideas and pick those you want to use in your story. Put them in order so your story has a beginning (explaining the situation), a middle (telling what everyone did), and an end (showing how the election turned out and how everyone felt about it).

**Step Three:** Write your story in sentences.
A. Include at least six of these words: release, elect, loan, coax, cheat, screen, vote, decrease, code, goal.
B. Use adjectives and adverbs to help explain what happens.
C. Use specific words instead of general ones.
D. Use both "plain" verbs and the **-ing** forms (with **is, are, was,** or **were**).

**Step Four:** Read your story out loud to a partner and listen while your partner reads his or hers. Are both stories clear? Did either of you leave anything out? Did you use specific words?

**Step Five:** Make any needed changes and rewrite your story below. Give it a title. Use more paper if you need it. Maybe your teacher will post the stories on the wall or bulletin board so you can read each others' and find out what happened in all the elections.

___stories will vary___

_____

_____

_____

_____

_____

_____

_____

_____

_____

Copyright © 1991 American Education Publishing Co.    24

---

## Spelling Words With Digraphs

A digraph is two consonant letters pronounced as one consonant sound. Here are three digraphs: /sh/ as in shell, /ch/ as in chew, and /th/ as in thin.

**Directions:** Write in **sh, ch,** or **th** to complete each word below.

1. _th_ reaten
2. _ch_ ill
3. _sh_ ock
4. _sh_ iver
5. _th_ aw
6. _ch_ allenge
7. peri _sh_
8. _sh_ ield
9. _ch_ art
10. _th_ rive

**Directions:** Finish these sentences with a word that contains the digraph given.

1. A trip to the South Pole would really be a /ch/ ___challenge___.

2. The ice there never /th/ ___thaws___ because the temperature averages -50 C.

3. How can any living thing /th/ ___thrive___ or even live when it's so cold?

4. With six months of total darkness and those icy temperatures, any plants would soon /sh/ ___perish___.

5. Even the thought of that numbing cold makes me /sh/ ___shiver___.

6. The cold and darkness /th/ ___threaten___ the lives of explorers.

7. The explorers take along maps and /ch/ ___charts___ to help them find their way.

8. Special clothing helps protect and /sh/ ___shield___ them from the cold.

9. Still, the weather must be a /sh/ ___shock___ at first.

10. Did someone leave a door open? Suddenly I feel a /ch/ ___chill___.

25    Copyright © 1991 American Education Publishing Co.

---

## Choosing "Joining Words"

Too many short sentences make writing seem choppy, but we can combine some of these sentences with "joining words."

**Directions:** Use one of the "joining words" given to combine each pair of sentences.

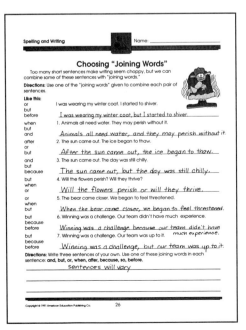

**Like this:**
or
but
before    I was wearing my winter coat. I started to shiver.
     ___I was wearing my winter coat, but I started to shiver.___

when
but
and    1. Animals all need water. They may perish without it.
     ___Animals all need water, and they may perish without it.___

after
or
but    2. The sun came out. The ice began to thaw.
     ___After the sun came out, the ice began to thaw.___

and
but
because    3. The sun came out. The day was still chilly.
     ___The sun came out, but the day was still chilly.___

but
when
or    4. Will the flowers perish? Will they thrive?
     ___Will the flowers perish or will they thrive.___

or
when
but    5. The bear came closer. We began to feel threatened.
     ___When the bear came closer, we began to feel threatened.___

but
because
before    6. Winning was a challenge. Our team didn't have much experience.
     ___Winning was a challenge because our team didn't have much experience.___

but
because
before    7. Winning was a challenge. Our team was up to it.
     ___Winning was a challenge, but our team was up to it.___

**Directions:** Write three sentences of your own. Use one of these joining words in each sentence: and, but, or, when, after, because, so, before.

___sentences will vary___

_____

_____

Copyright © 1991 American Education Publishing Co.    26

## Cracking The Code

**Directions:** Each symbol below stands for a consonant letter. Write the letters on the lines under each symbol. Then add vowels to spell words from the word box.

| challenge | shock | thaw | chart | threaten | perish | chill | shiver | thrive | shield |

| ☆ | + | O | X | Σ | □ | ◇ | △ | § | ≠ | Ø | π | = |
|---|---|---|---|---|---|---|---|---|---|---|---|---|
| c | d | g | h | k | l | n | p | r | s | t | v | w |

**Like this:**

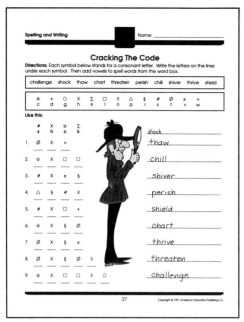

| ≠ | X | ☆ | Σ |
|---|---|---|---|
| s | h | c | k |

shock

1. Ø X =    thaw

2. ☆ X □ □    chill

3. ≠ X π §    shiver

4. △ § ≠ X    perish

5. ≠ X □ +    shield

6. ☆ X π Ø    chart

7. Ø X π    thrive

8. Ø X § Ø ◇    threaten

9. ☆ X □ □ ◇ O    challenge

---

## Combining Ideas

When two sentences repeat some of the same information, we often can combine them into one sentence with fewer words.

**Directions:** Combine each set of sentences into one sentence. Some will have two subjects, some will have two verbs, and some will be joined with words such as **when, before, but,** or **because**.

**Like this:** The sun came out. The river started to thaw. The pond also thawed.

When the sun came out, the river and pond started to thaw.

1. The rain continued for days. The river flooded. The river threatened to cover the roads.
When the rain continued for days, the river flooded and threatened to cover the roads.

2. The catcher shivered in the cold morning air. The batter shivered, too. They had forgotten their jackets.
The catcher and batter shivered in the cold morning air because they had forgotten their jackets.

3. I talked to my plants. I watered them every day. They still died.
I talked to my plants and watered them every day, but they still died.

4. Germs thrive on dirty hands. Bacteria thrive, too. They both multiply there.
Germs and bacteria thrive and multiply on dirty hands.

**Directions:** Write your own sentences, following the instructions.   sentences will vary

1. Write a sentence with two subjects:

2. Write a sentence with two verbs:

3. Write a sentence with two subjects and two verbs:

---

## Searching For Synonyms

**Directions:** Circle a word or a phrase in each sentence that is a synonym for a word in the word box. Write the synonym from the word box on the line.

| challenge | shock | thaw | chart | threaten | perish | chill | shiver | thrive | shield |

**Like this:** The writing was in an old code.   ancient

1. A fish out of water will quickly die.   perish
2. The ice carving is beginning to melt.   thaw
3. I was amazed when I saw how he looked.   shocked
4. The puppy was trembling with excitement.   shivering
5. Ferns need moisture to grow well.   thrive
6. Are you trying to scare me?   threaten
7. Let the salad get cold in the refrigerator.   chill
8. She tried to protect him from the truth.   shield
9. He made a list of different kinds of birds.   chart
10. They dared us to enter the contest.   challenged

**Directions:** Write your own sentences for five words from the word box to prove you know what they mean. (If you're not sure, look them up in a dictionary.) Trade your sentences with someone else. Do you think that person understands the words he or she used in sentences?

Sentences will vary

---

## Knowing When To Stop

Although we can combine some of our short sentences, we also need to know when to end a sentence and start a new one.

**Directions:** Use periods, question marks, and exclamation marks to show where sentences should end in these paragraphs. Circle the first letter in the first word of each new sentence to show it should be a capital letter.

The farmers were worried about their orange crop. Temperatures that night were supposed to reach a record low. The chill might stop the buds on the trees from developing into oranges. The drop in temperature threatened to ruin the entire year's crop.

On our last camping trip I was really glad to have my new sleeping bag. The other campers were shivering in their sleeping bags, but mine had a special lining that shielded me from the cold. The next morning I noticed ice on a puddle starting to thaw. I was shocked! I really had been cold that night. Thank goodness for my new sleeping bag!

**Directions:** Some of the periods in the paragraphs below are in the wrong place. Rewrite each paragraph, putting periods where they belong and combining some of the shorter sentences.

The Antarctic Circle. Is the area around the South Pole. Days there are six months long. Nights are also six months long. When it is day at the South Pole. It is night at the North Pole.

The Antarctic Circle is the area around the South Pole. Days and nights are six months long. When it is day at the South Pole, it is night at the North Pole.

Some people think tourists should not go into the Antarctic Circle. Because they disturb the animals that live there. Tours tend to take place. At the same time the penguins begin their breeding season. The seals also breed then. Sometimes the animals leave the breeding areas. When they feel threatened by tourists. They are also scared of the tourists' helicopters.

Some people think tourists should not go into the Antarctic Circle because they disturb the animals that live there. Tours tend to take place at the same time the penguins and seals begin their breeding season. Sometimes the animals leave the breeding areas when they feel threatened by tourists and their helicopters.

---

## Practicing Proofreading

**Directions:** Circle the six spelling and pronoun mistakes in each paragraph. Write the words correctly on the lines below. (Some words are from earlier lessons. If you have trouble spelling them, look on page 1, 9, 17, or 25.)

Julie always braged about being ready to meet any chalenge or reach any gole. When it was time for our class to elekt it's new officers, Julie said we should voat for her to be president.

bragged    challenge    goal
elect    its    vote

Gary wanted to be ours president, too. He tried to coaks everyone to vote for his! He even lowned kids money to get their votes! Well, Julie may have too much pryde in herself, but I like her in spit of that. At least she didn't try to buy our votes!

our    coax    him
loaned    pride    spite

Its true that Julie tried other ways to get us to vote for hers. She scrubbed the chalkboards even though it was Peter's job for that week. One day I saw her rinseing out the paint brushes when it was Peter's turn to do it. Then she made sure we knew about her good deeds so we would praize her.

It's    her    scrubbed
daily    rinsing    praise

We had the election, but I was shalked when the teacher releaseed the results. Gary won! I wondered if her cheated somehow. I feel like our class was robed! Now Gary is the one who's braging about how great he is. I wish he knew the titel of president doesn't mean anything I or one wants to be around you!

shocked    released    cheated
robbed    bragging    title

---

## Review

The temperature at the North Pole averages -20 to -30 degrees F in the winter and approaches the melting point only during June, July, and August. Snow and ice cover the land the rest of the year, and the seas are choked with ice. The first people to reach the North Pole, U.S. explorers Robert E. Peary and Matthew Henson, traveled there by dog sled in 1909. Many other explorers died trying to reach this spot.

**Directions:** Write a story about something that might have happened as Peary and Henson struggled to the North Pole so long ago. Were they threatened by any dangerous animals? (Polar bears live and hunt at the North Pole.) Did they have any trouble with their dogs or their food supply or the weather? Use your own paper if necessary.

**Follow these steps:**
**Step One:** Write all your ideas for a story on another sheet of paper. Then pick the ones you want to use and put them in order.
**Step Two:** Write your story in sentences on another sheet of paper.
**A.** Include at least six of these words: challenge, shock, thaw, chart, threaten, perish, chill, shiver, thrive, shield.
**B.** Combine some of your short sentences using joining words.
**C.** Use periods, questions marks, exclamation marks, and capital letters in your sentences.
**Step Three:** Read your story out loud to a partner. Help each other by suggesting changes that will make your stories easier to understand. Is it clear what happened in your stories?
**Step Four:** Rewrite your story in the space below. Use more paper if you need it. If you want, draw a picture to go with it. Perhaps your teacher will have a few students read their stories every day so you can all enjoy the imaginary adventures of Peary and Henson.

Stories will vary

## Spelling sh Different Ways

The digraph /sh/ is often spelled with the letters **sh**, but it can also be spelled **s** as in sure, **ss** as in pressure, **ci** as in special, **ti** as in protection, and **si** as in possession.

**Directions:** Use words from the word box in these exercises.

| decision | division | pressure | addition | ancient |
| subtraction | confusion | multiplication | social | correction |

1. Write each word in the row with the letters that spell its /sh/ sound.

**ss** <u>pressure</u> _____

**si** <u>division</u>   <u>confusion</u>   <u>decision</u>

**ci** <u>ancient</u>   <u>social</u>

**ti** <u>addition</u>   <u>subtraction</u>   <u>multiplication</u>   <u>correction</u>

2. Finish each word by filling in the missing letters that spell the /sh/ sound.

deci <u>si</u> on   so <u>ci</u> al   subtrac <u>ti</u> on   an <u>ci</u> ent   confu <u>si</u> on

addi <u>ti</u> on   pre <u>ss</u> ure   multiplica <u>ti</u> on   correc <u>ti</u> on   divi <u>si</u> on

3. Write in the word that finishes each sentence. Use each word from the word box only once.

1 + 2 is an example of _____ <u>addition</u>

6 - 4 is an example of _____ <u>subtraction</u>

10 ÷ 2 is an example of _____ <u>division</u>

2 x 6 is an example of _____ <u>multiplication</u>

When you decide something, you make a _____ <u>decision</u>

Something very old is _____ <u>ancient</u>

A mistake can be the result of some _____ <u>confusion</u>

---

## Putting Ideas In Order

**Directions:** Read each topic sentence and the ideas below it. Then put the ideas in order and write a paragraph for each topic. At least one idea doesn't belong with the rest in the same paragraph. Cross it out and don't include it in your paragraph. You can add other words or sentences to the paragraph, as long as you stay on the same topic. Begin sentences with capital letters and end them with periods, question marks, or exclamation marks. (Don't keep repeating "they" in your second paragraph. Think of other words to use.)

**Like this:**  Topic sentence: Whales are more like people than fish.
Ideas: breathe through lungs
have skin, not scales
can drown
air goes out through blowhole
used to be hunted and killed

**Whales are more like people than fish. They have skin instead of scales like fish. They also breathe through lungs like people and can drown if they stay under water too long. They breathe through a blowhole in the top of their heads.**

Topic sentence: Addition is not difficult to do.
Ideas: write the answer under the line
add the third number to that
here is how to add three numbers
my math teacher is Mr. Herman
first, write the numbers in a column and put a line under the last one
then start at the top and add the first two numbers

Addition is not difficult to do. Here is how to add three numbers. First, write the numbers in a column and put a line under the last one. Then start at the top and add the first two numbers. Add the third number to that. Write the answer under the line.
Omit: my math teacher is Mr. Herman.

---

## Writing Support Sentences For A Topic

A paragraph is a group of sentences that tell about one topic. The topic sentence in a paragraph usually is first and tells the main idea of the paragraph. Support sentences follow and provide details about the same topic.

**Directions:** Write at least three support sentences for each topic sentence below. Use your imagination, but make sure each of your sentences is on the same topic. (Some sentences offer a choice of topics. Underline the one you like best and write about it.)

**Like this:**
Carly had an accident on her bike. She was on her way to the store to buy some bread. A car came weaving down the road and scared her. She rode her bike off the road so the car wouldn't hit her. Now her knee is scraped, but she's all right.

*support sentences will vary*

I've been thinking of ways I could make some money after school.
_____
_____

In my opinion, cats (or dogs or fish) make the best pets.
_____
_____

My life would be better if I had (a younger sister, a younger brother, an older sister, or an older brother).
_____
_____

I'd like to live next door to a (swimming pool or video store or movie theater).
_____
_____

---

## Meeting Word Families

A word family is a group of words based on the same word. For example, **playful**, **playground**, and **playing** are all based on the word **play**.

**Directions:** Use words from the word box in these exercises.

| decision | division | pressure | addition | ancient |
| subtraction | confusion | multiplication | social | correction |

1. Write the word from the word box that belongs to the same word family as each one below.

correctly   <u>correction</u>   confused   <u>confusion</u>

divide   <u>division</u>   subtracting   <u>subtraction</u>

pressing   <u>pressure</u>   society   <u>social</u>

multiply   <u>multiplication</u>   decide   <u>decision</u>

added   <u>addition</u>   ancestor   <u>ancient</u>

2. Complete each sentence by writing the correct form of the word given. Remember to drop the final **e** on verbs before adding **-ing** or **-ed**.

**Like this:**
Have you (decide) <u>decided</u> what to do? Did you make a (decide) <u>decision</u> yet?

I am (add) <u>adding</u> the numbers right now. Would you check my (add) <u>addition</u>?

This problem has me (confuse) <u>confused</u>. Can you clear up my (confuse) <u>confusion</u>?

This is a (press) <u>pressing</u> problem. We feel (press) <u>pressure</u> to solve it right away.

Is he (divide) <u>dividing</u> by the right number? Will you help him with his (divide) <u>division</u>?

Try to answer (correct) <u>correctly</u>. Then you won't have to make any (correct) <u>corrections</u> on your paper later on.

I am (multiply) <u>multiplying</u> by 43. Maybe I should look at the (multiply) <u>multiplication</u> tables.

I already (subtract) <u>subtracted</u> six from ten. Are there any more (subtract) <u>subtraction</u> problems to do?

---

## Sounding Out Syllables

A syllable is a word or part of a word with only one vowel. For example, **boat** has one syllable, **to-tie** has two syllables, **re-mem-ber** has three syllables, and **ex-pe-ri-ence** has four syllables.

**Directions:** Use words from the word box in these exercises.

| decision | division | pressure | addition | ancient |
| subtraction | confusion | multiplication | social | correction |

1. Write each word from the word box in the row that tells how many syllables it has.

Two: <u>pressure</u>   <u>social</u>   <u>ancient</u>

Three: <u>decision</u>   <u>division</u>   <u>addition</u>   <u>subtraction</u>
<u>confusion</u>   <u>correction</u>

Five: <u>multiplication</u>

2. Write in the missing syllables for each word.

<u>so</u> cial   sub <u>trac</u> tion   mul <u>ti</u> pli <u>ca</u> tion   pre <u>ssure</u>

di <u>vi</u> sion   an <u>cient</u>   deci <u>sion</u>   add <u>i</u> tion

<u>con</u> fusion   cor <u>rec</u> tion

3. Beside each word below, write a word from the word box with the same number of syllables. Use each word from the word box only once.

daily   <u>any 2-syllable word</u>   challenging   <u>any 3-syllable word</u>

syllable   <u>any 3-syllable word</u>   election   <u>any 3-syllable word</u>

decreasing   <u>any 3-syllable word</u>   threaten   <u>any 2-syllable word</u>

advantage   <u>any 3-syllable word</u>   shivering   <u>any 3-syllable word</u>

title   <u>any 2-syllable word</u>   experimenting   <u>multiplication</u>

---

## Building Paragraphs

**Directions:** Read each group of questions and the topic sentence. On another sheet of paper, write support sentences that answer each question. Use your imagination! Put the support sentences in order and copy them on this page after the topic sentence. Trade your paragraphs with someone else. How are your paragraphs the same? How are they different?

**Questions:** What was her decision?   Why did she decide that? Why was the decision hard to make?

On her way home from school, Mariko made a difficult decision.
*paragraphs will vary*
_____
_____
_____

**Questions:** What was the confusion about?   How was Charlie involved in it? What did he do to clear it up?

Suddenly, Charlie thought of a way to clear up all the confusion.
_____
_____
_____

**Questions:** Why did Beth feel awkward before?   How does she feel now? What happened to change the way she feels?

Beth used to feel awkward at the school social activities.
_____
_____
_____

Name: _____

## Using Plurals In Math

To make most nouns plural, we just add **s**. Except: When a noun ends with **s, ss, sh, ch,** or **x,** we add **es**: bus, buses; cross, crosses; brush, brushes; church, churches; box, boxes. When a noun ends with a consonant and **y,** we change the **y** to **i** and add **es**: berry, berries. The spelling of some plural words changes without adding **s**: man, men; mouse, mice.

**Directions:** Write in the correct plural or singular form of the words in these math problems. Write whether the problem requires addition, subtraction, multiplication, or division. Solve the problem!

**Like this:**

3 (mouse) __mice__ + 1 (mouse) __mouse__ = Type of problem: __addition__

1. 3 (box) __boxes__ - 2 (box) __boxes__ = Type of problem: __subtraction__
2. 2 (supply) __supplies__ + 5 (supply) __supplies__ = Type of problem: __addition__
3. 4 (copy) __copies__ x 2 __copies__ = Type of problem: __multiplication__
4. 6 (class) __classes__ ÷ 2 __classes__ = Type of problem: __division__
5. 5 (factory) __factories__ - 3 (factory) __factories__ = Type of problem: __subtraction__
6. 3 (daisy) __daisies__ x 3 __daisies__ = Type of problem: __multiplication__
7. 8 (sandwich) __sandwiches__ + 4 (sandwich) __sandwiches__ = Type of problem: __addition__
8. 3 (child) __children__ - 1 (child) __child__ = Type of problem: __subtraction__
9. 10 (brush) __brushes__ ÷ 5 __brushes__ = Type of problem: __division__
10. 4 (goose) __geese__ + 1 (goose) __goose__ = Type of problem: __addition__

---

Name: _____

## Writing Similes And Metaphors

We can describe something by using adjectives and adverbs. As you know, adjectives describe nouns and tell what kind or how many. Adverbs tell about verbs and explain where, how, how much, or how often. (See page 18 to review adjectives and adverbs.)

ADJ     ADV
**Like this:** The frightened girl huddled in a corner.

We can also describe things by comparing them to something else. (If we use **like** or **as,** our comparison is called a simile.)

**Like this:** She looked **like** a frightened mouse.

If we don't use **like** or **as,** the comparison is called a metaphor.

**Like this:** She was a frightened mouse.

**Directions:** Rewrite each of these sentences two ways to make them more interesting. The first time (A), add at least one adjective and one adverb. The second time (B), compare something in the sentence to something else, using a simile or metaphor.

**Like this:** The baby cried.

A. _The sick baby cried softly all night._

B. _The baby cried louder and louder, like a storm gaining strength._

1. The stranger arrived.

A. _sentences will vary_

B. _____

2. She has an imagination.

A. _____

B. _____

3. The statue was beautiful.

A. _____

B. _____

4. The furniture was comfortable.

A. _____

B. _____

---

Name: _____

## Review

**Directions:** Think about the ways you use — or will use — addition, subtraction, multiplication, and division in your daily life. Decide which of the four you think is — or will be — the most valuable for you. Which do you think will be the least valuable? Now write **two** paragraphs below. In the first one, explain why you think one of the ways to work with numbers, addition for example, is or will be important in your life. In the second paragraph, tell why you think you won't need one of the ways, maybe division, very often. To write your paragraphs, follow these steps:

**Step One:** On another sheet of paper write down all your reasons why one form of arithmetic is useful to you. On a second sheet, write why another form may not be as useful. Read over your ideas, select the ones you want to use for each paragraph, and put them in order.

**Step Two:** Write both paragraphs in sentences on still another sheet of paper.
A. Begin each paragraph with a topic sentence and add details to support sentences.
B. Include at least six of these words in your paragraphs: decision, division, pressure, addition, ancient, subtraction, confusion, multiplication, social, correction.
C. Use at least six plural nouns, spelled correctly.

**Step Three:** Read your paragraphs to a partner. Do all the sentences belong where you put them? Would a different order make the sentences easier to understand?

**Step Four:** Rewrite both paragraphs in the space below. Use more paper if you need it. Or write them on a separate sheet of paper so your teacher can post everyone's opinions on a bulletin board and you can read each others'.

_paragraphs will vary_

_____
_____
_____
_____
_____
_____
_____
_____

---

Name: _____

## Adding Missing Syllables

**Directions:** Write in the missing syllables for these words. Then write how many syllables each word has. The words in the word box will help with spelling.

| statue | imagination | jealous | future | arrangement |
|---|---|---|---|---|
| furniture | stranger | project | justice | capture |

**Like this:**

syl _l_ a ble (3)     _w o r k_ book (2)

pro _j e c t_ (2)     ar _r a n g e_ ment (3)     _c a p_ ture (2)

_s t a_ tue (2)     furni _t u r e_ (3)     _j u s_ tice (2)

stran _g e r_ (2)     i magina _t i o n_ (5)     jeal _o u s_ (2)

_f u_ ture (2)

**Directions:** Circle both spelling errors in each sentence and write the words correctly on the lines. Some words are from earlier lessons.

1. You'll need (imajnation) to complete this (projeck).
   _imagination_  _project_

2. Do you like the (tile) of this new (furnichure)?
   _style_  _furniture_

3. Does your (stachue) have a (titel)?
   _statue_  _title_

4. I made an (arrangment) to repay my (lone).
   _arrangement_  _loan_

5. The (stranjer) seemed to have made a (dicision).
   _stranger_  _decision_

6. I admit I felt (jealus) when she got so much (praze).
   _jealous_  _praise_

7. He (robed) the bank, but he still deserves (justise).
   _robbed_  _justice_

---

Name: _____

## Spelling Words With /j/ And /ch/

The /j/ sound can be spelled with a **j** as in jump, with **g** before **e** or **i** as in age and giant, or as **ge** at the end of words such as page. The /ch/ sound is often spelled with the letters **ch,** but it can be spelled with a **t** before **u,** as in nature.

**Directions:** Use the words from the word box in these exercises.

| statue | imagination | jealous | future | arrangement |
|---|---|---|---|---|
| furniture | stranger | project | justice | capture |

1. Say each word in the word box and then write it in the correct row, depending on whether it has a /j/ or a /ch/ sound.

/j/ __imagination__ __jealous__ __arrangement__
__stranger__ __project__ __justice__

/ch/ __statue__ __future__ __furniture__ __capture__

2. Write a word from the word box that belongs to the same word family as each one below.

imagine __imagination__     arranging __arrangement__
strongely __stranger__     furnish __furniture__
just __justice__     jealousy __jealous__

3. Finish each sentence with a word containing the sound given.

What is your group's /j/ __project__ this week?

The sheriff is no /j/ __stranger__ to /j/ __justice__.

She used her /j/ __imagination__ to solve the problem.

My sister keeps rearranging the /f/ __furniture__ in our room.

---

Name: _____

## Reaching Out To Readers

We can create a picture in our readers' minds by telling them how something looks, sounds, feels, smells, or tastes. For example, compare A and B below. Notice how the description in B makes you imagine how the heavy door and the cobweb would feel and how the broken glass would look and sound as someone walked on it.

A. I walked into the house.
B. I pushed open the heavy wooden door of the old house. A cobweb brushed my face and broken glass, sparkling like ice, crunched under my feet.

**Directions:** Write one or two sentences about each topic below. Add details that will help your reader see, hear, smell, or taste what you are describing, like B above. Adjectives, adverbs, similes, and metaphors will help you create a picture.

1. Your favorite dinner cooking
   _sentences will vary_

2. Old furniture
   _____

3. Wind blowing in the trees
   _____

4. A tired stranger
   _____

5. Wearing wet clothes
   _____

6. A strange noise somewhere in the house
   _____

7. Making something from wet clay
   _____

## Page 45 — Seeking Synonyms

# Seeking Synonyms

**Directions:** Circle a word or group of words in each sentence that is a synonym for a word in the word box. Write the synonym from the word box on the line.

| statue | imagination | jealous | future | arrangement |
|--------|-------------|---------|--------|-------------|
| furniture | stranger | project | justice | capture |

Like this:   She will (lend) me her book.   _loan_

1. He tried to (catch) the butterfly.   _capture_
2. No one knows what will happen in the (time to come).   _future_
3. They are loading the (chairs and tables and beds) into the moving van.   _furniture_
4. We almost finished our team (assignment).   _project_
5. They made (plans) to have a class party.   _arrangements_
6. Kenny made a (model) of a horse.   _statue_
7. The accused man asked the judge for (fairness).   _justice_

**Directions:** Write your own sentences for these words: stranger, imagination, and jealous. Then pick two other words from the word box and use them in sentences. Make each sentence at least ten words long and prove you know what the word means.

1. _sentences will vary_
2. _____
3. _____
4. _____
5. _____

---

## Page 46 — Writing A Picture

# Writing A Picture

**Directions:** For each topic sentence below, write three or four support sentences. Include details about how things look, sound, smell, taste, or feel to help readers feel as if they are right there. Don't forget to use adjectives, adverbs, similes, and metaphors.

**Like this:** After my dog had his bath, I couldn't believe how much better he looked. His fur that used to be all matted and dirty was as clean as new snow. He still felt a little damp when I scratched behind his ears. The stink from rolling in our garbage was gone, too. He smelled like apples now because of the shampoo.

1. My little cousin's birthday party was almost over.
   _supporting sentences will vary_

2. I always keep my grandpa company while he bakes bread.

3. By the end of our day at the beach, I was a mess.

4. Early morning is the best time to go for a bike ride.

5. I like to go to the grocery store.

---

## Page 47 — Spelling Crossing Words

# Spelling Crossing Words

**Directions:** Figure out the word that matches each definition and write it in the spaces that begin with the same number. (If you need help thinking of the words or spelling them, look on page 41.)

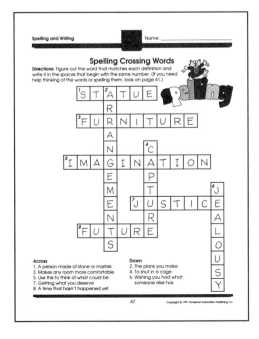

Crossword answers:
- 1 ACROSS: STATUE
- 3 ACROSS: FURNITURE
- 5 ACROSS: IMAGINATION
- 7 ACROSS: JUSTICE
- 8 ACROSS: FUTURE
- 2 DOWN: ARRANGEMENTS
- 4 DOWN: CAPTURE
- 6 DOWN: JEALOUSY

**Across**
1. A person made of stone or marble
3. Makes any room more comfortable
5. Use this to think of what could be
7. Getting what you deserve
8. A time that hasn't happened yet

**Down**
2. The plans you make
4. To shut in a cage
6. Wishing you had what someone else has

---

## Page 48 — Review

# Review

**Directions:** Follow the steps below to write at least two paragraphs describing a place at school, at home, in your neighborhood, or in your community. Don't name it, but describe it in such detail that your reader will know where it is. It might be the art room at school, your bedroom at home, or the corner store. Then trade your description with someone else and see if you each can guess what the other person described.

**Follow these steps to write your paragraphs:**
**Step One:** Decide on a place to write about and list on another sheet of paper everything you would see, hear, feel, smell, or even taste there. Select the ideas you will use.
**Step Two:** Write your paragraphs in sentences on another sheet of paper.
**A.** Start each paragraph with a topic sentence. One paragraph might tell what you would see there, and the second paragraph might describe what you would hear or feel or smell.
**B.** Try to include three of these words in your writing: statue, imagination, jealous, future, arrangement, furniture, stranger, project, justice, capture.
**C.** Use many adjectives and adverbs and at least one simile and one metaphor.
**Step Three:** Read your paragraphs out loud to yourself. Did you include enough details so your reader will recognize the place you described? (Remember not to mention the name of the place.)
**Step Four:** Copy your description below. Use more paper if you need it. Then trade with someone. Can you figure out what he or she is describing? Tell your partner what you like about the description he or she wrote.

_descriptions will vary_

---

## Page 49 — Spelling Words With The /ou/ and /oi/ Vowels

# Spelling Words With The /ou/ and /oi/ Vowels

The /ou/ sound can be spelled ou as in pound or ow as in power. The /oi/ sound can be spelled oi as in oil or oy as in boy.

**Directions:** Use words from the word box to complete the exercises.

| doubt   amount   avoid   annoy   announce   choice   poison   powder   soil   however |
|---|

1. Write each word in the row that names at least one of its vowel sounds.

/ou/   _doubt_   _amount_   _announce_   _powder_   _however_

/oi/   _avoid_   _annoy_   _choice_   _poison_   _soil_

2. Write in the letters that spell the missing /ou/ or /oi/ vowel sound in each word.

d **ou** bt   p **oi** son   ch **oi** ce   am **ou** nt   h **ow** ever

av **oi** d   ann **oy**   p **ow** der   s **oi** l   ann **ou** nce

3. Finish these sentences by writing in a word with the vowel sound given. Use each word from the word box only once.

When is the principal going to /ou/ _announce_ the winners?

Since it hasn't rained, the /oi/ _soil_ in our garden is as dry as/ou/ _powder_ .

We wanted a different one, but we didn't have any /oi/ _choice_ .

I have no /ou/ _doubt_ that you will do your best.

She did tell us, /ou/ _however_ , that she might be late.

After you add the numbers, please tell me the total /ou/ _amount_ .

I haven't seen you lately. Are you trying to /oi/ _avoid_ me?

Do you know the phone number of the nearest /oi/ _poison_ control center?

I think you just said that to /oi/ _annoy_ me.

---

## Page 50 — Separating Facts From Opinions

# Separating Facts From Opinions

A fact is a true statement, something that can be proved.
Here is a fact: A poodle is a breed of dog.
An opinion is what someone thinks or believes.
Here is an opinion: Poodles make the best pets.
We can use both facts and opinions in our writing, but we need to recognize which is which.

**Directions:** Write F beside the facts and O beside the opinions.

_F_ 1. Many cleaning products are poison if they are swallowed.
_F_ 2. Poisons can kill babies and small children.
_O_ 3. Anyone who keeps poison cleaning products at home doesn't care about children.
_O_ 4. Most cleaning products shouldn't even be sold to people who have young children.
_F_ 5. Keeping cleaning products locked up is one way to keep children safe.
_F_ 6. Our teacher assigned topics for our science reports.
_O_ 7. We really should have a choice of topics.
_O_ 8. If we could choose what we wanted to write about, we'd all pick good topics.
_F_ 9. Most young people in grade five have some kind of hobby or other interest.
_O_ 10. If we could learn more about our hobbies, we'd write better reports.

**Directions:** Write one fact and one opinion about the same topic. Then read them to a partner. Does your partner agree with you on which sentence is a fact and which is an opinion?

Fact: _will vary_

Opinion: _will vary_

## Page 51

### Meeting New Word Families

Remember that a word family is a group of words based on the same word, like care, caring, and careful.

**Directions:** Use words from the word box in these exercises.

| doubt amount avoid annoy announce choice poison powder soil however |

1. Write the word from the word box that belongs to the same word family as each one below.

| avoidance | _avoid_ | annoyance | _annoy_ |
| doubtful | _doubt_ | soiled | _soil_ |
| announcement | _announce_ | poisonous | _poison_ |
| choose | _choice_ | amounted | _amount_ |
| powdery | _powder_ | whenever | _however_ |

2. Complete each sentence by writing in the correct form of the word given. Remember to drop the final **e** on verbs before adding -**ing** or -**ed**.

**Like this:**
Are you (doubt) _doubting_ my word? You never (doubt) _doubted_ it before.

The teacher is (announce) _announcing_ the next test. Did you hear what he (announce) _announced_ ?

This stream was (poison) _poisoned_ by a chemical from a factory nearby.

Is the chemical (poison) _poisoning_ any other water supply? How many (poison) _poisons_ does the factory produce?

My cat always (annoy) _annoys_ our dog.

Last night she (annoy) _annoyed_ him for hours.

I think Carrie is (avoid) _avoiding_ me. Yesterday she (avoid) _avoided_ walking home with me.

51

## Page 52

### Supporting An Opinion

**Directions:** Decide what your opinion is on each topic below. Then write a paragraph supporting your opinion. Begin with a topic sentence that tells the reader what you think. Add details in the next three or four sentences that show why you are right.

**Like this:** Whether kids should listen to music while they do homework
**Kids do a better job on their homework if they listen to music. The music makes the time more enjoyable. It also drowns out the sounds of the rest of the family. If things are too quiet while kids do homework, every little sound distracts them.**

1. Whether young people should have a choice about going to school, no matter how old they are
   _Support paragraphs vary_

2. Whether all parents should give their children the same amount of money for an allowance

3. Whether you should tell someone if you doubt he or she is telling the truth

52

## Page 53

### Listening For Sounds

**Directions:** Not every word spelled with **ow** is pronounced /ou/. Circle the words below that have the /ou/ sound.

yellow (coward) glow (vowel) lower (towel) (down)
sparrow (powerful) snowstorm bowl (brown) know (now)
fellow (flower) (growl) growth knowledge (shower) flow

**Directions:** In the same way, not every word spelled with **ou** is pronounced /ou/. The letters **ou** can be pronounced a number of ways. Circle the words below that have the /ou/ sound.

touch (sour) nervous (south) source tough (scout) tour
precious (country) (account) (counter) cough (pouch) court
doughnut (bound) could curious pour (council) bought

**Directions:** Write the word from the word box that rhymes with each of these words or phrases. Some words are used twice.

| doubt amount avoid annoy announce choice poison powder soil however |

| joys and | _poison_ | two counts | _announce_ |
| shout | _doubt_ | loyal | _soil_ |
| a boy | _annoy_ | crowd her | _powder_ |
| employed | _avoid_ | Joyce | _choice_ |
| now never | _however_ | a count | _amount_ |
| voice | _choice_ | employ | _annoy_ |
| a bounce | _announce_ | louder | _powder_ |
| enjoyed | _avoid_ | trout | _doubt_ |

53

## Page 54

### Considering Different Opinions

People often have different opinions about the same thing. Each of us has a different "point of view."

**Directions:** Both topic sentences below are the same. Write the rest of each paragraph from the point of view of the person named. (Write two or three sentences that tell how that person would feel about the Reds winning the game.)

Terry, a player for the Reds in the last second of the basketball game between the Reds and the Cowboys, the Reds scored and won the game.

_paragraph completions will vary_

Chris, a player for the Cowboys in the last second of the basketball game between the Reds and the Cowboys, the Reds scored and won the game.

**Directions:** Here's a different situation. Write these paragraphs from three points of view: Katie, her dad, and her brother.

**Katie**
Katie's dog had chewed up another one of her father's shoes.

**Katie's father**
Katie's dog had chewed up another one of her father's shoes.

**Katie's brother Mark, who would rather have a cat**
Katie's dog had chewed up another one of her father's shoes.

54

## Page 55

### Finding The Spelling Mistakes

**Directions:** Circle the spelling mistakes in each paragraph. Write the words correctly on the lines below. If you need help spelling any of the words, look on page 1, 9, 17, 25, 33, 41, or 49.

Some poisons that kill insects can also threaten people. Often these powders and sprays are used on corn, beans, and other plants we eat. Unless these plants are well scrubbed we may eat a small amount of the poison.

_poisons_ _threaten_ _powders_ _scrubbed_ _amount_

Sometimes the poison is put in the soil and moves into the plant through its roots. Then it stays in the plant in spite of all our rinsing. All we can do is avoid eating food that has been grown this way. However, that also means we have to expect more insects in our food. It's a hard choice. Some people doubt that a little bit of poison will hurt them, while others have made a decision to grow their own food.

_soil_ _spite_ _rinsing_ _avoid_ _however_
_it's_ _choice_ _doubt_ _poison_ _decision_

One day a stranger came into the corner store while I was there stocking up on candy bars. The man held out a dollar and asked for change. Well, the next thing I knew, he was robbing the store! He grabbed some money from the clerk's hand. I was so shocked I just stood there like a statue.

_stranger_ _stocking_ _robbing_ _shocked_ _statue_

Maybe it was my imagination but I thought he had a gun in his pocket. A chill went down my back. Just then a police car pulled up outside with it lights flashing. The clerk must have flipped a silent alarm. Justice was on its way!

_imagination_ _chill_ _its_ _flipped_ _justice_

Yesterday the teacher announced a new project. She challenged us to think of a new arrangement for the furniture in the room. We voted to put the chairs in groups. Then Brian said it would be easier to cheat that way. I was annoyed I told him we had more pride than that! (I thought about punching him to prove it!)

_announced_ _project_ _challenged_ _arrangement_ _furniture_
_voted_ _cheat_ _annoyed_ _pride_ _punching_

55

## Page 56

### Review

**Directions:** Write about the use of poison to kill insects on food crops from the point of view of a company that makes the poison and from the point of view of a person concerned about the effects of the poison on people. To get started, reread the first two paragraphs on page 55.

**Then follow these steps:**
**Step One:** On another sheet of paper, write "the company's point of view" and list all the reasons the company might give for farmers to use poison to kill insects on their food crops (tomatoes, corn, wheat, and so on). What might insects do to a crop? Would people buy that food? On a second sheet of paper, write "concerned citizen's point of view." List reasons someone might not want farmers to use poison to kill insects on these crops. (You might also want to do some research on this topic.) Then put the ideas on each page in order to make one or two paragraphs from each point of view.
**Step Two:** Write each paragraph (or two) in sentences on another sheet of paper.
A. Start each paragraph with a topic sentence.
B. Include at least six of these words: doubt, amount, avoid, annoy, announce, choice, poison, powder, soil, however.
**Step Three:** Read your paragraphs over and see if each one is as convincing as it can be, from opposite points of view. Make any necessary changes.
**Step Four:** Copy each point of view below, using more paper if you need it.

From the company's point of view:
_paragraphs will vary_

From a concerned citizen's point of view:

56

## Spelling Words With Silent Letters

Some letters in words are not pronounced, such as the s in island, the t in listen, the k in knee, the h in hour, and the w in write.

**Directions:** Use words from the word box for these exercises.

| wrinkle honest aisle knife wrist rhyme exhaust glisten knowledge wrestle |
| --- |

1. Write each word beside its silent letter. (One word has two silent letters, so write it twice.)

s __aisle__

t __glisten__  __wrestle__

h __honest__  __rhyme__  __exhaust__

w __wrinkle__  __wrist__  __wrestle__

k __knife__  __knowledge__

2. This time, write in the missing letter for each word.

w res _t_ le      ex _h_ aust      _k_ nife      glis _t_ en      ai _s_ le

_k_ nowledge      _w_ rinkle      r _h_ yme      _h_ onest      _w_ rist

3. Finish these sentences by writing in a word with the silent letter given. Use each word from the word box only once.

He always tells the truth. He's very (h) __honest__ .

In an airplane I like to sit in the seat closest to the (s) __aisle__ .

I need a sharper (k) __knife__ to cut this bread.

I have a feeling that long hike is going to (h) __exhaust__ me.

Did you sleep in that shirt? It has so many (w) __wrinkles__ !

The snow seemed to (t) __glisten__ in the sunlight.

To play tennis, you need a strong (w) __wrist__ .

57

Copyright © 1991 American Education Publishing Co.

---

## Writing A Longer Report

**Directions:** Write a six-paragraph description of the town or city where you live, following these steps:

**Step One:** Under each heading below, write everything you know about that topic. Write facts for the first three topics and your opinion for the last three. The information under topic 1 will be an introduction to your town. Topics 2 through 5 will be the body of your report. Topic 6 will be your ending or conclusion.

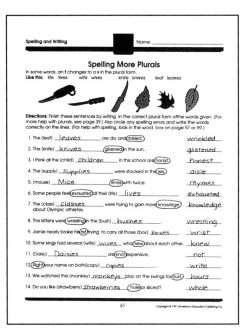

1. The name of my town and what it looks like      __answers vary__

_____

2. The types of people who live here (ages, what kinds of work they do, and so on)

_____

3. The kinds of businesses that are here

_____

4. The best thing about this town

_____

5. One thing I'd like to change

_____

6. How I feel about living here

_____

**Step Two:** Now put the ideas under each topic in order and write a paragraph for each one on another sheet of paper. Use adjectives and adverbs in your description and choose specific words to "paint a picture" of your town. If possible, include a simile or metaphor, comparing your town to something else.

**Step Three:** Read your report to a partner and listen to his or hers. How are your reports different? Is anything important missing from one of them? Remember, they don't have to be the same because you each have your own point of view.

**Step Four:** Make any necessary changes and copy your report on a clean sheet of paper. Draw a picture to go with it, if you like. Maybe your teacher will combine all the reports in a book titled Our Town (or City).

Copyright © 1991 American Education Publishing Co.      60

---

## Organizing Several Paragraphs

**Directions:** The ideas below are all about the sport of wrestling, but there is too much information for one paragraph. Read the two topics for the paragraphs. Then put a number in front of each idea to show which paragraph it should go in.

1. Wrestling in ancient Greece
2. Wrestling today

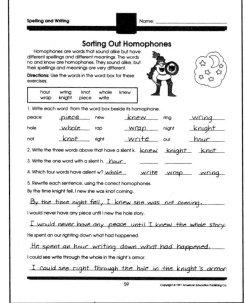

_1_ wrestling common in Greek myths and on Greek vases and coins

_2_ now wrestlers earn points for being in control of the other person

_1_ wrestling was the most popular sport among ancient Greeks

_2_ today wrestling in the schools has rules to prevent injury and encourage the wrestlers to develop skill and concentration

_1_ one type of Greek wrestling involved knocking the other man down

_2_ wrestling is popular in high schools and colleges today

**Directions:** Now put the ideas for each paragraph in order and write the paragraphs in sentences on another sheet of paper. Add words or make any other necessary changes so your paragraphs will be clear. Then copy your paragraphs on the lines below. Be sure to use periods and capital letters in your sentences.

Wrestling was the most popular sport among ancient Greeks. It was common in their myths and was shown on vases and coins. The Greeks had two kinds of wrestling. In one type, the winner just had to knock the other man down.

Wrestling is still popular in high schools and colleges today, but rules prevent injury and encourage the wrestlers to develop skill and concentration. The can earn points just for being in control of the other wrestler.

paragraphs may vary from examples given

Copyright © 1991 American Education Publishing Co.      58

---

## Spelling More Plurals

In some words, an f changes to a v in the plural form.
Like this:  life  lives    wife  wives    knife  knives    leaf  leaves

**Directions:** Finish these sentences by writing in the correct plural form of the words given. (For more help with plurals, see page 39.) Also circle any spelling errors and write the words correctly on the lines. (For help with spelling, look in the word box on page 57 or 59.)

1. The (leaf) __leaves__ are dry and (rinkled.)      __wrinkled__

2. The (knife) __knives__ (glisened) in the sun.      __glistened__

3. I think all the (child) __children__ in this school are (honist)      __honest__

4. The (supply) __supplies__ were stacked in the (isle)      __aisle__

5. (mouse) __Mice__ (rimes) with twice.      __rhymes__

6. Some people feel (exausted) all their (life) __lives__      __exhausted__

7. The (class) __classes__ were trying to gain more (knowlege) about Olympic athletes.      __knowledge__

8. The kittens were (wresling) in the (bush) __bushes__      __wrestling__

9. Jamie nearly broke his (rist) trying to carry all those (box) __boxes__      __wrist__

10. Some kings had several (wife) __wives__ who (new) about each other.      __knew__

11. (Daisy) __Daisies__ are (knot) expensive.      __not__

12. (Right) your name on both (copy) __copies__      __write__

13. We watched the (monkey) __monkeys__ play on the swings for (ours.)      __hours__

14. Do you like (strawberry) __strawberries__ (hole) or sliced?      __whole__

61      Copyright © 1991 American Education Publishing Co.

---

## Sorting Out Homophones

Homophones are words that sound alike but have different spellings and different meanings. The words no and know are homophones. They sound alike, but their spellings and meanings are very different.

**Directions:** Use the words in the word box for these exercises.

| hour  wring  knot  whole  knew |
| wrap  knight  piece  write |

1. Write each word from the word box beside its homophone.

peace __piece__      new __knew__      ring __wring__

hole __whole__      rap __wrap__      night __knight__

not __knot__      right __write__      our __hour__

2. Write the three words above that have a silent k. __knew__ __knight__ __knot__

3. Write the one word with a silent h. __hour__

4. Which four words have silent w? __whole__ __write__ __wrap__ __wring__

5. Rewrite each sentence, using the correct homophones.

By the time knight fell, I new she was knot coming.

__By the time night fell, I knew she was not coming.__

I would never have any piece until I new the hole story.

__I would never have any peace until I knew the whole story.__

He spent an our righting down what had happened.

__He spent an hour writing down what had happened.__

I could see write through the whole in the night's armor.

__I could see right through the hole in the knight's armor.__

59      Copyright © 1991 American Education Publishing Co.

---

## Review

**Directions:** Do you remember everything you learned in this workbook? See if you can answer all the questions below.

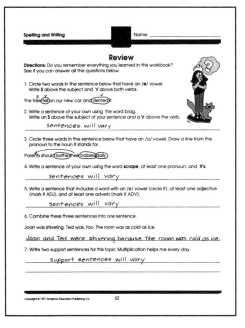

1. Circle two words in the sentence below that have an /e/ vowel. Write S above the subject and V above both verbs.

The tree (fell) on our new car and (dented) it.

2. Write a sentence of your own using the word brag. Write an S above the subject of your sentence and a V above the verb.

__sentences will vary__

3. Circle three words in the sentence below that have an /a/ vowel. Draw a line from the pronoun to the noun it stands for.

Parents should (bathe) their (babies) (daily.)

4. Write a sentence of your own using the word scrape, at least one pronoun, and it's.

__sentences will vary__

5. Write a sentence that includes a word with an /e/ vowel (circle it), at least one adjective (mark it ADJ), and at least one adverb (mark it ADV).

__sentences will vary__

6. Combine these three sentences into one sentence.

Joan was shivering. Ted was, too. The room was as cold as ice.

__Joan and Ted were shivering because the room was as cold as ice.__

7. Write two support sentences for this topic: Multiplication helps me every day.

__support sentences will vary__

62

# The MASTER SKILLS SERIES

*Workbooks for all the basic skills children need to succeed!*

Master
English

Grades K-6

Master
Math

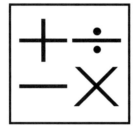

Grades K-6

Master
Reading

Grades K-6

Master
Comprehension

Grades 1-6

Master
Study Skills

Grades 1-6

Master
Spelling & Writing

Grades 1-6

**Grade K workbooks include 30 lessons plus answer key.**
**Grades 1-6 workbooks include 62 lessons plus answer key.**

# NOTES

# NOTES

# NOTES

# END OF ANSWER KEY

Dear Friend:

**A**merican Education Publishing is dedicated to designing and developing the highest quality learning materials at the most affordable prices.

The cornerstone of our efforts is a commitment to children and their need for the highest quality education in a competitive world. Our children are the primary asset in America's future. We must provide them with the skills to enrich our proud heritage.

We view the profession of teaching and the responsibility of parenting with the greatest esteem. To ensure that all children experience successful learning requires the involvement and cooperation of home, school, business and the entire community.

It is the objective of American Education Publishing to provide the educational materials and help foster an environment in which students:

✎ Start school and each grade level prepared and ready to learn.

✎ Consistently improve their skill levels in challenging subject matter.

✎ Value and respect the education process and increase their desire for learning.

✎ Gain a level of preparedness for responsible citizenship, further learning and world competition.

Thank you for your dedication to young people.

Name: _____

# Practicing Proofreading

**Directions:** Circle the six spelling and pronoun mistakes in each paragraph. Write the words correctly on the lines below. (Some words are from earlier lessons. If you have trouble spelling them, look on page 1, 9, 17, or 25.)

Julie always braged about being ready to meet any chalenge or reach any gole. When it was time for our class to elekt it's new officers, Julie said we should voat for her to be president.

_____ _____ _____

_____ _____ _____

Gary wanted to be ours president, too. He tried to coaks everyone to vote for his. He even lowned kids money to get their votes!  Well, Julie may have too much pryde in herself, but I like her in spit of that. At least she didn't try to buy our votes!

_____ _____ _____

_____ _____ _____

Its true that Julie tried other ways to get us to vote for hers. She scrubed the chalkboards even though it was my dayly job for that week. One day I saw her rinseing out the paint brushes when it was Peter's turn to do it. Then she made sure we knew about her good deeds so we would praize her.

_____ _____ _____

_____ _____ _____

We had the election, but I was shalked when the teacher releaseed the results. Gary won! I wondered  if he cheeted somehow. I feel like our class was robed! Now Gary is the one who's braging about how great he is. I wish he knew the titel of president doesn't mean anything if no one wants to be around you!

_____ _____ _____

_____ _____ _____

# Review

The temperature at the North Pole averages -20 to -30 degrees F in the winter and approaches the melting point only during June, July, and August. Snow and ice cover the land the rest of the year, and the seas are choked with ice. The first people to reach the North Pole, U.S. explorers Robert E. Peary and Matthew Henson, traveled there by dog sled in 1909. Many other explorers died trying to reach this spot.

**Directions:** Write a story about something that might have happened as Peary and Henson struggled to the North Pole so long ago. Were they threatened by any dangerous animals? (Polar bears live and hunt at the North Pole.) Did they have any trouble with their dogs or their food supply or the weather? Use your own paper if necessary.

**Follow these steps:**

**Step One:** Write all your ideas for a story on another sheet of paper. Then pick the ones you want to use and put them in order.

**Step Two:** Write your story in sentences on another sheet of paper.

**A.** Include at least six of these words: challenge, shock, thaw, chart, threaten, perish, chill, shiver, thrive, shield.

**B.** Combine some of your short sentences using joining words.

**C.** Use periods, questions marks, exclamation marks, and capital letters in your sentences.

**Step Three:** Read your story out loud to a partner. Help each other by suggesting changes that will make your stories easier to understand. Is it clear what happened in your stories?

**Step Four:** Rewrite your story in the space below. Use more paper if you need it. If you want, draw a picture to go with it. Perhaps your teacher will have a few students read their stories every day so you can all enjoy the imaginary adventures of Peary and Henson.

_____

_____

_____

_____

_____

Name: _____

# Spelling sh Different Ways

The digraph /sh/ is often spelled with the letters **sh**, but it can also be spelled **s** as in **s**ure, **ss** as in pre**ss**ure, **ci** as in spe**ci**al, **ti** as in protec**ti**on, and **si** as in posse**ssi**on.

**Directions:** Use words from the word box in these exercises.

| decision subtraction | division confusion | pressure multiplication | addition social | ancient correction |
|---|---|---|---|---|

1. Write each word in the row with the letters that spell its /**sh**/sound.

**ss** _____ _____ _____ _____

**si** _____ _____ _____ _____

**ci** _____ _____ _____ _____

**ti** _____ _____ _____ _____

2. Finish each word by filling in the missing letters that spell the /**sh**/ sound.

deci __ __ on    so __ __ al    subtrac __ __ on    an __ __ ent    confu __ __ on

addi __ __ on    pre __ __ ure    multiplica __ __ on    correc __ __ on    divi __ __ on

3. Write in the word that finishes each sentence. Use each word from the word box only once.

1 + 2 is an example of _____.

6 - 4 is an example of _____.

10 ÷ 2 is an example of _____.

2 x 6 is an example of _____.

When you decide something, you make a _____.

Something very old is _____.

A mistake can be the result of some _____.

Name: _____

# Writing Support Sentences For A Topic

A paragraph is a group of sentences that tell about one topic. The topic sentence in a paragraph usually is first and tells the main idea of the paragraph. Support sentences follow and provide details about the same topic.

**Directions:** Write at least three support sentences for each topic sentence below. Use your imagination, but make sure each of your sentences is on the same topic. (Some sentences offer a choice of topics. Underline the one you like best and write about it.)

**Like this:**
Carly had an accident on her bike. She was on her way to the store to buy some bread. A car came weaving down the road and scared her. She rode her bike off the road so the car wouldn't hit her. Now her knee is scraped, but she's all right.

I've been thinking of ways I could make some money after school.

_____

_____

_____

In my opinion, cats (or dogs or fish) make the best pets.

_____

_____

_____

My life would be better if I had (a younger sister, a younger brother, an older sister, or an older brother).

_____

_____

_____

I'd like to live next door to a (swimming pool or video store or movie theater).

_____

_____

_____

Name: _____

# Sounding Out Syllables

A syllable is a word or part of a word with only one vowel. For example, **boat** has one syllable, **ta-ble** has two syllables, **re-mem-be**r has three syllables, and **ex-pe-ri-ence** has four syllables.

**Directions:** Use words from the word box in these exercises.

| | | | | |
|---|---|---|---|---|
| decision | division | pressure | addition | ancient |
| subtraction | confusion | multiplication | social | correction |

1. Write each word from the word box in the row that tells how many syllables it has.

Two: _____    _____    _____    _____

Three: _____    _____    _____    _____

_____    _____    _____    _____

Five: _____    _____    _____    _____

2. Write in the missing syllables for each word.

__ __ cial          sub __ __ __ __ tion          mul __ __ pli __ __ tion          pre __ __ __ __ __

di __ __ sion       an __ __ __ __ __              deci __ __ __ __                   ad __ __ tion

__ __ __ fusion     cor __ __ __ tion

3. Beside each word below, write a word from the word box with the same number of syllables. Use each word from the word box only once.

daily _____           challenging _____

syllable _____         election _____

decreasing _____       threaten _____

advantage _____        shivering _____

title _____            experimenting _____

Name: _____

# Putting Ideas In Order

**Directions:** Read each topic sentence and the ideas below it. Then put the ideas in order and write a paragraph for each topic. At least one idea doesn't belong with the rest in the same paragraph. Cross it out and don't include it in your paragraph. You can add other words or sentences to the paragraph, as long as you stay on the same topic. Begin sentences with capital letters and end them with periods, question marks, or exclamation marks. (Don't keep repeating "they" in your second paragraph. Think of other words to use.)

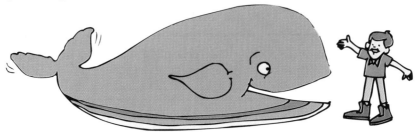

**Like this:**    Topic sentence:    Whales are more like people than fish.
                 Ideas:             breathe through lungs
                                    have skin, not scales
                                    can drown
                                    air goes out through blowhole
                                    used to be hunted and killed

**Whales are more like people than fish. They have skin like people instead of scales like fish. They also breathe through lungs like people and can drown if they stay under water too long. They breathe through a blowhole in the top of their heads.**

Topic sentence:    Addition is not difficult to do.
Ideas:             write the answer under the line
                   add the third number to that
                   here is how to add three numbers
                   my math teacher is Mr. Herman
                   first, write the numbers in a column and put a line under the last one
                   then start at the top and add the first two numbers

_____

_____

_____

_____

**Spelling and Writing**

Name: _____

# Meeting Word Families

A word family is a group of words based on the same word. For example, **playful**, **playground**, and **playing** are all based on the word **play**.

**Directions:** Use words from the word box in these exercises.

| decision | division | pressure | addition | ancient |
|---|---|---|---|---|
| subtraction | confusion | multiplication | social | correction |

1. Write the word from the word box that belongs to the same word family as each one below.

correctly     _____     confused     _____

divide     _____     subtracting     _____

pressing     _____     society     _____

multiply     _____     decide     _____

added     _____     ancestor     _____

2. Complete each sentence by writing the correct form of the word given. Remember to drop the final **e** on verbs before adding **-ing** or **-ed**.

**Like this:**

Have you (decide) __decided__ what to do? Did you make a (decide) __decision__ yet?

I am (add) _____ the numbers right now. Would you check my (add)_____ ?

This problem has me (confuse) _____ . Can you clear up my (confuse) _____ ?

This is a (press) _____ problem. We feel (press) _____ to solve it right away.

Is he (divide) _____ by the right number? Will you help him with his (divide) _____ ?

Try to answer (correct) _____ . Then you won't have to make any (correct)_____ on your paper later on.

I am (multiply) _____ by 43. Maybe I should look at the (multiply) _____ tables.

I already (subtract) _____ six from ten. Are there any more (subtract) _____ problems to do?

37

Copyright © 1991 American Education Publishing Co.

Name: _____

# Building Paragraphs

**Directions:** Read each group of questions and the topic sentence. On another sheet of paper, write support sentences that answer each question. Use your imagination! Put the support sentences in order and copy them on this page after the topic sentence. Trade your paragraphs with someone else. How are your paragraphs the same? How are they different?

**Questions:** - What was her decision?      Why did she decide that?
Why was the decision hard to make?

On her way home from school, Mariko made a difficult decision.

_____

_____

_____

_____

**Questions:** What was the confusion about?      How was Charlie involved in it?
What did he do to clear it up?

Suddenly, Charlie thought of a way to clear up all the confusion.

_____

_____

_____

_____

**Questions:** Why did Beth feel awkward before?      How does she feel now?
What happened to change the way she feels?

Beth used to feel awkward at the school social activities.

_____

_____

_____

_____

Name: _____

# Using Plurals In Math

To make most nouns plural, we just add s. Except: When a noun ends with **s, ss, sh, ch**, or **x**, we add **es**: bus, bus**es**; cross, cross**es**; brush, brush**es**; church, church**es**; box, box**es**. When a noun ends with a consonant and **y**, we change the **y** to **i** and add **es**: berry, ber**ries**. The spelling of some plural words changes without adding **s**: man, men; mouse, mice.

**Directions:** Write in the correct plural or singular form of the words in these math problems. Write whether the problem requires addition, subtraction, multiplication, or division. Solve the problem!

**Like this:**

3 (mouse) ___mice___ + 1 (mouse) ___mouse___ = Type of problem: ___addition___

1. 3 (box) _____ - 2 (box) _____ = Type of problem: _____

2. 2 (supply) _____ + 5 (supply) _____ = Type of problem: _____

3. 4 (copy) _____ x 2 _____ = Type of problem: _____

4. 6 (class) _____ ÷ 2 _____ = Type of problem: _____

5. 5 (factory) _____ - 3 (factory) _____ = Type of problem: _____

6. 3 (daisy) _____ x 3 _____ = Type of problem: _____

7. 8 (sandwich) _____ + 4 (sandwich) _____ = Type of problem: _____

8. 3 (child) _____ - 1 (child) _____ = Type of problem: _____

9. 10 (brush) _____ ÷ 5 _____ = Type of problem: _____

10. 4 (goose) _____ + 1 (goose) _____ = Type of problem: _____

Name: _____

# Review

**Directions:** Think about the ways you use — or will use — addition, subtraction, multiplication, and division in your daily life. Decide which of the four you think is — or will be — the most valuable for you. Which do you think will be the least valuable? Now write two paragraphs below. In the first one, explain why you think one of the ways to work with numbers, addition for example, is or will be important in your life. In the second paragraph, tell why you think you won't need one of the ways, maybe division, very often. To write your paragraphs, follow these steps:

**Step One:** On another sheet of paper write down all your reasons why one form of arithmetic is useful to you. On a second sheet, write why another form may not be so useful. Read over your ideas, select the ones you want to use for each paragraph, and put them in order.

**Step Two:** Write both paragraphs in sentences on still another sheet of paper.

**A.** Begin each paragraph with a topic sentence and add details in support sentences.

**B.** Include at least six of these words in your paragraphs: decision, division, pressure, addition, ancient, subtraction, confusion, multiplication, social, correction.

**C.** Use at least six plural nouns, spelled correctly.

**Step Three:** Read your paragraphs to a partner. Do all the sentences belong where you put them? Would a different order makethe sentences easier to understand?

**Step Four:** Rewrite both paragraphs in the space below. Use more paper if you need it. Or write them on a separate sheet of paper so your teacher can post everyone's opinions on a bulletin board and you can read each others'.

_____

_____

_____

_____

_____

_____

_____

_____

Spelling and Writing

Name: _____

# Spelling Words With /j/ And /ch/

The /j/ sound can be spelled with a **j** as in **j**ump, with **g** before **e** or **i** as in a**ge** and **gi**ant, or as **ge** at the end of words such pa**ge**. The /**ch**/ sound is often spelled with the letters **ch**, but it can be spelled with a **t** before **u**, as in na**t**ure.

**Directions:** Use the words from the word box in these exercises.

| | | | | |
|---|---|---|---|---|
| statue | imagination | jealous | future | arrangement |
| furniture | stranger | project | justice | capture |

1. Say each word in the word box and then write it in the correct row, depending on whether it has a /j/ or a /ch/ sound.

/j/      _____   _____   _____   _____

          _____   _____   _____   _____

/ch/     _____   _____   _____   _____

2. Write a word from the word box that belongs to the same word family as each one below.

imagine      _____      arranging      _____

strangely    _____      furnish        _____

just         _____      jealousy       _____

3. Finish each sentence with a word containing the sound given.

What is your group's /j/ _____ this week?

The sheriff is no /j/ _____ to /j/ _____ .

She used her /j/ _____ to solve the problem.

My sister keeps rearranging the /t/ _____ in our room.

41

Copyright © 1991 American Education Publishing Co.

Name: _____

# Writing Similes And Metaphors

We can describe something by using adjectives and adverbs. As you know, adjectives describe nouns and tell what kind or how many. Adverbs tell about verbs and explain where, when, how, how much, or how often. (See page 18 to review adjectives and adverbs.)

                ADJ          ADV

**Like this:**    The <u>frightened</u> girl huddled <u>in a corner</u>.

We can also describe things by comparing them to something else. (If we use **like** or **as**, our comparison is called a simile.)

**Like this:**    She looked **like** a frightened mouse.

If we don't use **like** or **as**, the comparison is called a metaphor.

**Like this:**    She was a frightened mouse.

**Directions:** Rewrite each of these sentences two ways to make them more interesting. The first time (**A**), add at least one adjective and one adverb. The second time (**B**), compare something in the sentence to something else, using a simile or metaphor.

**Like this:**    The baby cried.

A. _____ The sick baby cried softly all night. _____

B. _____ The baby cried louder and louder, like a storm gaining strength. _____

1. The stranger arrived.

A. _____

B. _____

2. She has an imagination.

A. _____

B. _____

3. The statue was beautiful.

A. _____

B. _____

4. The furniture was comfortable.

A. _____

B. _____

Name: _____

# Adding Missing Syllables

**Directions:** Write in the missing syllables for these words. Then write how many syllables each word has. The words in the word box will help with spelling.

| statue | imagination | jealous | future | arrangement |
| furniture | stranger | project | justice | capture |

**Like this:**

syl <u>l</u> a ble ( <u>3</u> )    <u>w o r k</u> book ( <u>2</u> )

pro _ _ _ _ ( _ )    ar _ _ _ _ _ ment ( _ )    _ _ _ ture ( _ )

_ _ _ tue ( _ )    furni _ _ _ _ ( _ )    _ _ _ tice ( _ )

stran _ _ _ ( _ )    _ magina _ _ _ _ ( _ )    jeal _ _ _ ( _ )

_ _ ture ( _ )

**Directions:** Circle both spelling errors in each sentence and write the words correctly on the lines. Some words are from earlier lessons.

1. You'll need imajination to complete this projeck.

_____

2. Do you like the stile of this new furnichure?

_____

3. Does your stachue have a titel?

_____

4. I made an arangement to repay my lone.

_____

5. The stranjer seemed to have made a dicision.

_____

6. I admit I felt jealus when she got so much praize.

_____

7. He robed the bank, but he still deserves justise.

_____

Name: _____

# Reaching Out To Readers

We can create a picture in our readers' minds by telling them how something looks, sounds, feels, smells, or tastes. For example, compare A and B below. Notice how the description in B makes you imagine how the heavy door and the cobweb would feel and how the broken glass would look and sound as someone walked on it.

A. I walked into the house.

B. I pushed open the heavy wooden door of the old house. A cobweb brushed my face and broken glass, sparkling like ice, crunched under my feet.

**Directions:** Write one or two sentences about each topic below. Add details that will help your reader see, hear, feel, smell, or taste what you are describing, like B above. Adjectives, adverbs, similes, and metaphors will help you create a picture.

1. Your favorite dinner cooking

_____

_____

2. Old furniture

_____

_____

3. Wind blowing in the trees

_____

_____

4. A tired stranger

_____

_____

5. Wearing wet clothes

_____

_____

6. A strange noise somewhere in the house

_____

_____

7. Making something from wet clay

_____

_____

Name: _____

# Seeking Synonyms

**Directions:** Circle a word or group of words in each sentence that is a synonym for a word in the word box. Write the synonym from the word box on the line.

| statue | imagination | jealous | future | arrangement |
| furniture | stranger | project | justice | capture |

**Like this:**     She will (lend) me her book.          _loan_

1. He tried to catch the butterfly.          _____

2. No one knows what will happen in the time to come.     _____

3. They are loading the chairs and tables and beds into the moving van.          _____

4. We almost finished our team assignment.          _____

5. They made plans to have a class party.          _____

6. Kenny made a model of a horse.          _____

7. The accused man asked the judge for fairness.          _____

**Directions:** Write your own sentences for these words: stranger, imagination, and jealous. Then pick two other words from the word box and use them in sentences. Make each sentence at least ten words long and prove you know what the word means.

1. _____

_____

2. _____

_____

3. _____

_____

4. _____

_____

5. _____

_____

Name: _____

# Writing A Picture

**Directions:** For each topic sentence below, write three or four support sentences. Include details about how things look, sound, smell, taste, or feel to help readers feel as if they are right there. Don't forget to use adjectives, adverbs, similes, and metaphors.

**Like this:** After my dog had his bath, I couldn't believe how much better he looked. **His fur that used to be all matted and dirty was as clean as new snow. He still felt a little damp when I scratched behind his ears. The stink from rolling in our garbage was gone, too. He smelled like apples now because of the shampoo.**

1. My little cousin's birthday party was almost over.

_____

_____

_____

2. I always keep my grandpa company while he bakes bread.

_____

_____

_____

3. By the end of our day at the beach, I was a mess.

_____

_____

_____

4. Early morning is the best time to go for a bike ride.

_____

_____

_____

5. I like to go to the grocery store.

_____

_____

_____

Name: _____

# Spelling Crossing Words

**Directions:** Figure out the word that matches each definition and write it in the spaces that begin with the same number. (If you need help thinking of the words or spelling them, look on page 41.)

## Across
1. A person made of stone or marble
3. Makes any room more comfortable
5. Use this to think of what could be
7. Getting what you deserve
8. A time that hasn't happened yet

## Down
2. The plans you make
4. To shut in a cage
6. Wishing you had what someone else has

Name: _____

# Review

**Directions:** Follow the steps below to write at least two paragraphs describing a place at school, at home, in your neighborhood, or in your community. Don't name it, but describe it in such detail that your reader will know where it is. It might be the art room at school, your bedroom at home, or the corner store. Then trade your description with someone else and see if you each can guess what the other person described.

**Follow these steps to write your paragraphs:**

**Step One:** Decide on a place to write about and list on another sheet of paper everything you would see, hear, feel, smell, or even taste there. Select the ideas you will use.

**Step Two:** Write your paragraphs in sentences on another sheet of paper.

**A.** Start each paragraph with a topic sentence. One paragraph might tell what you would see there, and the second paragraph might describe what you would hear or feel or smell.

**B.** Try to include three of these words in your writing: statue, imagination, jealous, future, arrangement, furniture, stranger, project, justice, capture.

**C.** Use many adjectives and adverbs and at least one simile and one metaphor.

**Step Three:** Read your paragraphs out loud to yourself. Did you include enough details so your reader will recognize the place you described? (Remember not to mention the name of the place.)

**Step Four:** Copy your description below. Use more paper if you need it. Then trade with someone. Can you figure out what he or she is describing? Tell your partner what you like about the description he or she wrote.

_____

_____

_____

_____

_____

_____

_____

_____

Name: _____

# Spelling Words With The /ou/ and /oi/ Vowels

The /**ou**/ sound can be spelled **ou** as in p**ou**nd or **ow** as in p**ow**er. The /**oi**/ sound can be spelled **oi** as in **oi**l or **oy** as in b**oy**.

**Directions:** Use words from the word box to complete the exercises.

| doubt   amount   avoid   annoy   announce   choice   poison   powder   soil   however |

1. Write each word in the row that names at least one of its vowel sounds.

/ou/       _____   _____   _____   _____   _____

/oi/       _____   _____   _____   _____   _____

2. Write in the letters that spell the missing /ou/ or /oi/ vowel sound in each word.

d __ __ bt      p __ __ son      ch __ __ ce      am __ __ nt      h __ __ ever

av __ __ d      ann __ __      p __ __ der      s __ __ l      ann __ __ nce

3. Finish these sentences by writing in a word with the vowel sound given. Use each word from the word box only once.

When is the principal going to /ou/ _____ the winners?

Since it hasn't rained, the /oi/ _____ in our garden is as dry as /ou/ _____ .

We wanted a different one, but we didn't have any /oi/ _____ .

I have no /ou/ _____ that you will do your best.

She did tell us, /ou/ _____ , that she might be late.

After you add the numbers, please tell me the total /ou/_____ .

I haven't seen you lately. Are you trying to /oi/ _____ me?

Do you know the phone number of the nearest /oi/ _____ control center?

I think you just said that to /oi/ _____ me.

Name: _____

# Separating Facts From Opinions

A fact is a true statement, something that can be proved.
Here is a fact: A poodle is a breed of dog.

An opinion is what someone thinks or believes.
Here is an opinion: Poodles make the best pets.

We can use both facts and opinions in our writing, but we need to recognize which is which.

**Directions:** Write **F** beside the facts and **O** beside the opinions.

_____ 1. Many cleaning products are poison if they are swallowed.

_____ 2. Poisons can kill babies and small children.

_____ 3. Anyone who keeps poison cleaning products at home doesn't care about children.

_____ 4. Most cleaning products shouldn't even be sold to people who have young children.

_____ 5. Keeping cleaning products locked up is one way to keep children safe.

_____ 6. Our teacher assigned topics for our science reports.

_____ 7. We really should have a choice of topics.

_____ 8. If we could choose what we wanted to write about, we'd all pick good topics.

_____ 9. Most young people in grade five have some kind of hobby or other interest.

_____ 10. If we could learn more about our hobbies, we'd write better reports.

**Directions:** Write one fact and one opinion about the same topic. Then read them to a partner. Does your partner agree with you on which sentence is a fact and which is an opinion?

Fact: _____

Opinion: _____

Name: _____

# Meeting New Word Families

Remember that a word family is a group of words based on the same word, like care, caring, and careful.

**Directions:** Use words from the word box in these exercises.

| doubt amount avoid annoy announce choice poison powder soil however |
| --- |

1. Write the word from the word box that belongs to the same word family as each one below.

avoidance     _____     annoyance     _____

doubtful     _____     soiled     _____

announcement     _____     poisonous     _____

choose     _____     amounted     _____

powdery     _____     whenever     _____

2. Complete each sentence by writing in the correct form of the word given. Remember to drop the final **e** on verbs before adding -**ing** or -**ed**.

**Like this:**
Are you (doubt) ___doubting___ my word?  You never (doubt) ___doubted___ it before.

The teacher is (announce) _____ the next test. Did you hear what he

(announce) _____ ?

This stream was (poison) _____ by a chemical from a factory nearby.

Is the chemical (poison) _____ any other water supply? How many

(poison) _____ does the factory produce?

My cat always (annoy) _____ our dog.

Last night she (annoy) _____ him for hours.

I think Carrie is (avoid) _____ me. Yesterday she (avoid) _____

walking home with me.

Name: _____

# Supporting An Opinion

**Directions:** Decide what your opinion is on each topic below. Then write a paragraph supporting your opinion. Begin with a topic sentence that tells the reader what you think. Add details in the next three or four sentences that show why you are right.

**Like this:** Whether kids should listen to music while they do homework

**Kids do a better job on their homework if they listen to music. The music makes the time more enjoyable. It also drowns out the sounds of the rest of the family. If things are too quiet while kids do homework, every little sound distracts them.**

1. Whether young people should have a choice about going to school, no matter how old they are

_____

_____

_____

2. Whether all parents should give their children the same amount of money for an allowance

_____

_____

_____

3. Whether you should tell someone if you doubt he or she is telling the truth

_____

_____

_____

_____

Name: _____

# Listening For Sounds

**Directions:** Not every word spelled with **ow** is pronounced /ou/. Circle the words below that have the /**ou**/ sound.

| yellow | coward | glow | vowel | lower | towel | down |
|---|---|---|---|---|---|---|
| sparrow | powerful | snowstorm | bowl | brown | know | now |
| fellow | flower | growl | growth | knowledge | shower | flow |

**Directions:** In the same way, not every word spelled with **ou** is pronounced /**ou**/. The letters **ou** can be pronounced a number of ways. Circle the words below that have the /**ou**/ sound.

| touch | sour | nervous | south | source | tough | scout | tour |
|---|---|---|---|---|---|---|---|
| precious | country | account | counter | cough | pouch | court | |
| doughnut | bound | could | curious | pour | council | bought | |

**Directions:** Write the word from the word box that rhymes with each of these words or phrases. Some words are used twice.

| doubt amount avoid annoy announce choice poison powder soil however |
|---|

| joys and | _____ | two counts | _____ |
| shout | _____ | loyal | _____ |
| a boy | _____ | crowd her | _____ |
| employed | _____ | Joyce | _____ |
| how never | _____ | a count | _____ |
| voice | _____ | employ | _____ |
| a bounce | _____ | louder | _____ |
| enjoyed | _____ | trout | _____ |

# Considering Different Opinions

People often have different opinions about the same thing. Each of us has a different "point of view."

**Directions:** Both topic sentences below are the same. Write the rest of each paragraph from the point of view of the person named. (Write two or three sentences that tell how that person would feel about the Reds winning the game.)

Terry, a player for the Reds In the last second of the basketball game between the Reds and the Cowboys, the Reds scored and won the game.

_____

_____

Chris, a player for the Cowboys In the last second of the basketball game between the Reds and the Cowboys, the Reds scored and won the game.

_____

_____

**Directions:** Here's a different situation. Write these paragraphs from three points of view: Katie, her dad, and her brother.

**Katie**
Katie's dog had chewed up another one of her father's shoes.

_____

**Katie's father**
Katie's dog had chewed up another one of her father's shoes.

_____

_____

**Katie's brother Mark, who would rather have a cat**
Katie's dog had chewed up another one of her father's shoes.

_____

_____

# Finding The Spelling Mistakes

**Directions:** Circle the spelling mistakes in each paragraph. Write the words correctly on the lines below. If you need help spelling any of the words, look on page 1, 9, 17, 25, 33, 41, or 49.

Some poisions that kill insects can also threten people. Often these pouders and sprays are used on corn, beans, and other plantswe eat. Unless these plants are well scrubed, we may eat a small amont of the poison.

_____  _____  _____  _____

Sometimes the poison is put in the soyl and moves into the plant through its roots. Then it stays in the plant in spyte of all our rinseing. All we can do is avoyd eating food that has been grown this way. Howver, that also means we have to expect more insects in our food. Its a hard chioce! Some people dout that a little bit of poision will hurt them, while others have made a dicision to grow their own food.

_____  _____  _____  _____

_____  _____  _____  _____

One day a stranjer came into the corner store while I was there stokking up on candy bars. The man held out a dollar and asked for change. Well, the next thing I knew, he was robing the store! He grabbed some money from the clerk's hand. I was so shokked, I just stood there like a stachue.

_____  _____  _____  _____

Maybe it was my imajination, but I thought he had a gun in his pocket. A chil went down my back. Just then a police car pulled up outside with it's lights flashing. The clerk must have tiped a silent alarm! Justise was on its way!

_____  _____  _____  _____

Yesterday the teacher anownced a new projict. She chalenged us to think of a new arangement for the furnichure in the room. We voated to put the chairs in groups. Then Brian said it would be easier to cheet that way. I was annoyd. I told him we had more pryde than that! (I thought about punchhing him to prove it!)

_____  _____  _____  _____

_____  _____  _____  _____

Name: _____

# Review

**Directions:** Write about the use of poison to kill insects on food crops from the point of view of a company that makes the poison and from the point of view of a person concerned about the effectsof the poison on people. To get started, reread the first two paragraphs on page 55.

**Then follow these steps:**

**Step One:** On another sheet of paper, write "the company's point of view" and list all the reasons the company might give for farmers to use poison to kill insects on their food crops (tomatoes, corn, wheat, and so on). What might insects do to a crop? Would people buy that food? On a second sheet of paper, write "concerned citizen's point of view." List reasons someone might not want farmers to use poison to kill insects on these crops. (You might also want to do some research on this topic.) Then put the ideas on each page in order to make one or two paragraphs from each point of view.

**Step Two:** Write each paragraph (or two) in sentences on another sheet of paper.

**A.** Start each paragraph with a topic sentence.

**B.** Include at least six of these words: doubt, amount, avoid, annoy, announce, choice, poison, powder, soil, however.

**Step Three:** Read your paragraphs over and see if each one is as convincing as it can be, from opposite points of view. Make any necessary changes.

**Step Four:** Copy each point of view below, using more paper if you need it.

From the company's point of view:

_____

_____

_____

From a concerned citizen's point of view:

_____

_____

_____

_____

Name: _____

# Spelling Words With Silent Letters

Some letters in words are not pronounced, such as the **s** in i**s**land, the **t** in lis**t**en, the **k** in **k**nee, the **h** in **h**our, and the **w** in **w**rite.

**Directions:** Use words from the word box for these exercises.

| wrinkle honest aisle knife wrist rhyme exhaust glisten knowledge wrestle |
| --- |

1. Write each word beside its silent letter. (One word has two silent letters, so write it twice.)

s _____ _____ _____

t _____ _____ _____

h _____ _____ _____

w _____ _____ _____

k _____ _____ _____

2. This time, write in the missing letter for each word.

_ res _ le        ex _ aust        _ nife        glis _ en        ai _ le

_ nowledge      _ rinkle         r _ yme        _ onest         _ rist

3. Finish these sentences by writing in a word with the silent letter given. Use each word from the word box only once.

He always tells the truth. He's very (h) _____ .

On an airplane I like to sit in the seat closest to the (s) _____.

I need a sharper (k) _____ to cut this bread.

I have a feeling that long hike is going to (h) _____ me.

Did you sleep in that shirt? It has so many (w) _____ !

The snow seemed to (t) _____ in the sunlight.

To play tennis, you need a strong (w) _____ .

Name: _____

# Organizing Several Paragraphs

**Directions:** The ideas below are all about the sport of wrestling, but there is too much information for one paragraph. Read the two topics for the paragraphs. Then put a number in front of each idea to show which paragraph it should go in.

1. Wrestling in ancient Greece
2. Wrestling today

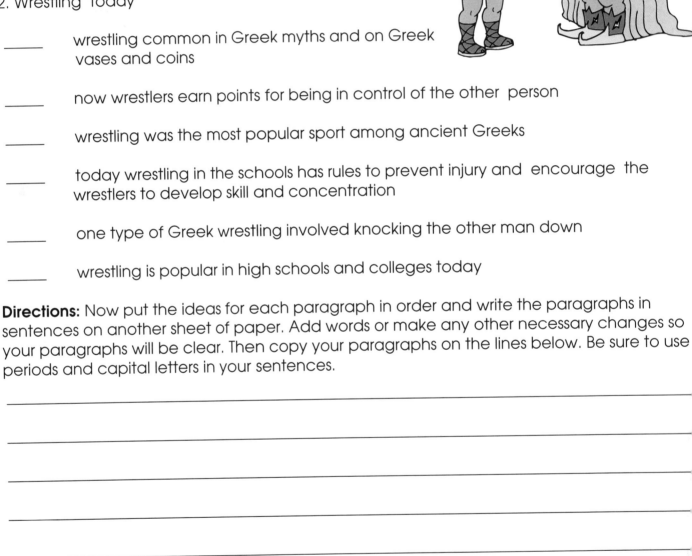

_____ wrestling common in Greek myths and on Greek vases and coins

_____ now wrestlers earn points for being in control of the other person

_____ wrestling was the most popular sport among ancient Greeks

_____ today wrestling in the schools has rules to prevent injury and encourage the wrestlers to develop skill and concentration

_____ one type of Greek wrestling involved knocking the other man down

_____ wrestling is popular in high schools and colleges today

**Directions:** Now put the ideas for each paragraph in order and write the paragraphs in sentences on another sheet of paper. Add words or make any other necessary changes so your paragraphs will be clear. Then copy your paragraphs on the lines below. Be sure to use periods and capital letters in your sentences.

_____

_____

_____

_____

_____

_____

_____

_____

Name: _____

# Sorting Out Homophones

Homophones are words that sound alike but have different spellings and different meanings. The words no and know are homophones. They sound alike, but their spellings and meanings are very different.

**Directions:** Use the words in the word box for these exercises.

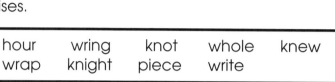

| hour | wring | knot | whole | knew |
|------|-------|------|-------|------|
| wrap | knight | piece | write | |

1. Write each word from the word box beside its homophone.

peace _____   new _____   ring _____

hole _____   rap _____   night _____

not _____   right _____   our _____

2. Write the three words above that have a silent k. _____  _____  _____

3. Write the one word with a silent h. _____  _____  _____

4. Which four words have a silent w? _____  _____  _____  _____

5. Rewrite each sentence, using the correct homophones.

By the time knight fell, I new she was knot coming.

_____

I would never have any piece until I new the hole story.

_____

We spent an our righting down what had happened.

_____

I could see write through the whole in the night's armor.

_____

Name: _____

# Writing A Longer Report

**Directions:** Write a six-paragraph description of the town or city where you live, following these steps:

**Step One:** Under each heading below, write everything you know about that topic. Write facts for the first three topics and your opinion for the last three. The information under topic 1 will be an introduction to your town. Topics 2 through 5 will be the body of your report. Topic 6 will be your ending or conclusion.

1. The name of my town and what it looks like

_____

2. The types of people who live here (ages, what kinds of work they do, and so on)

_____

3. The kinds of businesses that are here

_____

4. The best thing about this town

_____

5. One thing I'd like to change

_____

6. How I feel about living here

_____

**Step Two:** Now put the ideas under each topic in order and write a paragraph for each one on another sheet of paper. Use adjectives and adverbs in your description and choose specific words to "paint a picture" of your town. If possible, include a simile or metaphor, comparing your town to something else.

**Step Three:** Read your report to a partner and listen to his or hers. How are your reports different? Is anything important missing from one of them? Remember, they don't have to be the same because you each have your own point of view.

**Step Four:** Make any necessary changes and copy your report on a clean sheet of paper. Draw a picture to go with it, if you like. Maybe your teacher will combine all the reports in a book titled *Our Town (or City)*.

Name: _____

# Spelling More Plurals

In some words, an **f** changes to a **v** in the plural form.

**Like this:**   life   li**ves**      wife   wi**ves**        knife   kni**ves**      leaf   lea**ves**

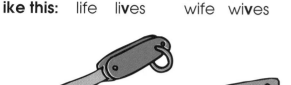

**Directions:** Finish these sentences by writing in the correct plural form of the words given. (For more help with plurals, see page 39.) Also circle any spelling errors and write the words correctly on the lines. (For help with spelling, look in the word box on page 57 or 59.)

1. The (leaf) _____ are dry and rinkled.                          _____

2. The (knife) _____ glisened in the sun..                     _____

3. I think all the (child) _____ in this school are honist.      _____

4. The (supply) _____ were stacked in the isle.               _____

5. (mouse) _____ rimes with twice.                             _____

6. Some people feel exausted all their (life) _____.           _____

7. The (class) _____ were trying to gain more knowlege        _____
   about Olympic athletes.

8. The kittens were wresling in the (bush) _____ .             _____

9. Jamie nearly broke his rist trying to carry all those (box) _____ . _____

10. Some kings had several (wife) _____ who new about each other.  _____

11. (Daisy) _____ are knot expensive.                          _____

12. Right your name on both (copy) _____ .                     _____

13. We watched the (monkey) _____ play on the swings for ours. _____

14. Do you like (strawberry) _____ hole or sliced?             _____

# Review

**Directions:** Do you remember everything you learned in this workbook? See if you can answer all the questions below.

1. Circle two words in the sentence below that have an /**e**/ vowel. Write **S** above the subject and **V** above both verbs.

The tree fell on our new car and dented it.

2. Write a sentence of your own using the word brag. Write an **S** above the subject of your sentence and a **V** above the verb.

_____

3. Circle three words in the sentence below that have an /a/ vowel. Draw a line from the pronoun to the noun it stands for.

Parents should bathe their babies daily.

4. Write a sentence of your own using the word **scrape**, at least one pronoun, and **it's**.

_____

5. Write a sentence that includes a word with an /e/ vowel (circle it), at least one adjective (mark it ADJ), and at least one adverb (mark it ADV).

_____

6. Combine these three sentences into one sentence.

Joan was shivering. Ted was, too. The room was as cold as ice.

_____

7. Write two support sentences for this topic: Multiplication helps me every day.

_____

_____